No sand dun

Memories of Wes

Edited by Robert Light

London League Publications Ltd

No sand dunes in Featherstone
Memories of West Yorkshire Rugby League
© The contributors. Foreword © David Hinchliffe, introduction and biographies of contributors © Robert Light.

Cover design © Stephen McCarthy.

Front cover: Billy Banks passes from the scrum: Huddersfield versus Halifax at Fartown 1953 (courtesy Robert Gate). Back cover: Thrum Hall: John Burnett scores for Halifax against Warrington in 1962 (courtesy Robert Gate). Title page: Yorkshire versus Lancashire at The Boulevard, 26 September 1956. Lancashire won 35–21. (Courtesy *Rugby League Journal*)

A CIP catalogue record for this book is available from the British Library.

First published in Great Britain in October 2010 by:
London League Publications Ltd, P.O. Box 10441, London E14 8WR

ISBN: 978-1903659-53-3

Cover design by: Stephen McCarthy Graphic Design
                            46, Clarence Road, London N15 5BB

Layout: Peter Lush

Printed in Great Britain by: MPG Books Group, Bodmin and King's Lynn

Foreword

This wonderful collection of rugby league memories offers not just a marvellously entertaining and often highly amusing read but, perhaps more significantly, also some unique insights into the history of the game and the communities within which it is played. This series of testimonies by a cross-section of former players, coaches, referees, fans and administrators of the game constitutes a commendable example of what oral histories can offer in terms of understanding the sociology of a sport and its place in society.

But while the student of social history or 20th century British sport will find much of importance within its pages, the book's content is as much a genuinely enjoyable read as a piece of serious academic research. There are wonderful tales of bizarre happenings, like the day Huddersfield RLFC somehow found themselves European champions. We hear of the amateur match, abandoned by the referee because of fighting, which resumed as a 'friendly' and was completed with no trouble at all. We're told of the role Leeds Cleansing Department played in the personal development of a former Great Britain coach and the day Don Fox was invited to appear at Sunday Night at the London Palladium. And to, cap it all, we learn that Mick Morgan is the product of a grammar school and I discover I can now boast that I know someone who once spoke to the French legend Jean Galia!

What comes over loud and clear from these stories is that rugby league's strength has always been its deep roots in close-knit local communities. We're told of the time when professional teams were primarily made up of players who lived and worked locally and Saturday afternoon's hero or villain on the field was back at his job at the Co-op Brush Works on Monday morning, being brought down to earth by the bloke on the next machine. We learn of the difficulties players faced getting time off for rugby league and how, when all professional players also had full-time employment outside the game, their sporting activities could also lead to lost jobs. It is difficult not to be left with a genuine admiration for the great personal commitment required by these part-time players in terms of the constant demands of regular training and match day routines. And while, at top level, today's Super League players have the luxury of being full-time, we shouldn't forget that nearly all the players in Championship One and Two are still part-timers facing perhaps not dissimilar pressures to those recalled in these memories.

This book records as well what happened when, at professional level, those in charge of the sport faced the wrath of its supporters when they overlooked rugby league's community roots and proposed ludicrous mergers of several famous, historic clubs. The tensions which occurred around the advent of Super League are recalled vividly in its pages.

There are reflections, too, on the nature of the modern game, with comparisons with the old unlimited tackle rule. While I have no personal doubt that we possess what is rightly called the Greatest Game, I do have some sympathy with several of the former players who ask whether contemporary rules have to some extent de-skilled the game and made it a little too predictable. The game's rulers at Red Hall would do well to note the thoughts of some of the wise old heads recorded here and look at some fine-tuning on the field so that you don't – as one former player suggests often "know what's going to happen."

The University of Huddersfield must be commended on establishing this oral history project and Robert Light is to be congratulated on both recording these remarkable memories and presenting them in a highly readable format. The end result is a very important piece of sporting literature.

David Hinchliffe
Holmfirth, September 2010

Acknowledgements
Any major research project such as the one upon which this book is based could not take place without the help of a considerable number of people. So I would like to first of all thank Dr Steve Kelly and Dr Peter Davies for having the initial idea, putting together the successful bid and giving me the opportunity to work on the project and the University of Huddersfield for providing the funding.

As project leader Steve also provided a great deal of help, support and encouragement throughout my time with the Centre for Oral History Research (COHR) at the University between 2007 and 2009. I was equally fortunate to be given similar support from Hilary Haigh, David Thorpe, Brian Haigh and Professor Tony Collins who were also members of the project steering committee. Gemma Robinson, Louise Hall, Ian Slattery, Dave Nichols, Craig Kemp, Danny Lancewicz, Ayden Anderson and John Seymour, all gave valuable assistance during work placements while studying at the University, as did David Holmes whose successful PhD study was also part of the project. Nick Kelly provided invaluable assistance with many of the transcriptions and as colleagues at the COHR Clare Jenkins, Nafhesa Ali and Chris Webb were constant sources of advice and support. I'd also like to thank Peter Lush and Dave Farrar for their considerable help and patience during the process of compiling the book and my family, Richard, Victoria and Isaac, and Frank and Marjorie. But most of all I'd like to thank all the people who we interviewed over the course of the project for their warmth, honesty insight and generosity. They have created a rich and important permanent record which will be appreciated by generations to come.
Robert Light

Robert Light and London League Publications Ltd would like to thank Steve McCarthy for designing the cover, Michael O'Hare for sub-editing, everyone who provided photographs for the book and the staff of MPG Biddles Ltd for printing the book.

Introduction

In September 2007 I was extremely fortunate to be given what many rugby league fans would describe as a dream job. I was appointed manager of the University of Huddersfield 'Up and Under' rugby league oral history project. Funded by an £85,000 internal grant, the project furthered the University's links with the rugby league community in West Yorkshire following its sponsorship deal with the Huddersfield Giants. As a lifelong fan of the game, I knew it would be an incredible opportunity to talk with some of the great players and coaches from the past I had read about or watched from the terraces, and hear the experiences of spectators with whom I had so much in common. But I wasn't fully aware of how far the interviews would reach beyond the game's history and offer deeper insights into life in Britain during the past 80 or so years.

They mostly took the form of life stories which reflected how rugby league had interacted with broader events in communities across West Yorkshire and beyond during this period. Almost every session began with an account of the interviewee's first memories of rugby league. So when I began to write the introduction to this book I reflected on my own early memories of the game. I grew up in the Yorkshire Dales, some distance from the traditional heartlands of rugby league. But my dad was a big sports fan and started taking my brother and me to watch Leeds in the early 1970s. I was only about five or six years old at the time and can recall virtually nothing of those early matches. But I do remember how a few years later we used to wait outside the members' bar at Headingley after the match for the *Green Final* to arrive. This also gave my dad and his mates the chance to go for a pint and it became part of our match day routine. We passed the time by playing on the cricket field, which you were allowed to do in those days. When the newspaper seller got to the ground we would set off for home. What stuck in my mind was how much I looked forward to reading through the report of the match we'd just seen. Even then I had become aware that media coverage of rugby league was scarce, especially where we lived, and the incredible skill, courage and excitement we witnessed was only accurately represented in local publications or the rugby league press. This feeling also reflected a view which came through in the memories of many fans we spoke to throughout the project, that rugby league has often been overlooked by the wider world.

In England, rugby league's image has been dominated by its close relationship with northern industrial working class regions in a way which has sometimes made the sport seem impenetrable to those elsewhere in the country. There is little doubt that the character of these communities and their cultural traditions also helped shaped the game's distinctive self image in a way that emphasises the importance of the project from which this collection has been drawn. Richard Hoggart highlighted how written accounts of life in industrial working class communities are often scarce and great emphasis has been placed on oral tradition as a means of preserving the past and making sense of its meaning in the present. Although the situation has improved considerably since, this lack of literary culture is reflected in the relative scarcity of books written about rugby league in comparison to other sports, especially before the start of the 1960s.

One of the great strengths of oral history, however, is the way it can give a voice to communities which are excluded from mainstream history by a lack of traditional written sources. The character of oral testimony can also provide more authentic and accessible accounts of history. Often in traditional narrative form, like the stories many of us were told by parents and grandparents we later wish had been recorded for posterity, such personal views of the past can bring to life characters and events that help develop a sense of family, community or sporting heritage. For as the historian Alessandro Portelli has explained: "History, we have been taught, is facts, actual and objective events you can touch and see; stories, in contrast, are the tales, the people who tell them, the words they are made of, the knot of memory and imagination that turns material facts into cultural meanings. Stories, in other words, communicate what history means to human beings." [1]

The aim of the 'Up and Under' rugby league oral history project was to 'preserve, celebrate and broaden recognition of the sport's rich social and cultural history in West Yorkshire'. It is hoped that this collection of extracts from the interviews we recorded will help to fulfil those aims. Unfortunately, it was not possible to include material from all of the 100 or so interviews which were recorded during the project. But that should not detract from the importance of those which are not included. The recollections of every person we talked to provide a valuable personal insight into the game's history. They will ultimately be made available to anyone interested in the history of the game and the communities in which it is played as part of the Rugby Football League Archive. A selection of audio clips from the interviews is available at the project website: www.rugbyleagueoralhistory.co.uk .

All bar one of the interviewees had a strong connection with some aspect of the game in West Yorkshire. The one exception was Bryn Knowelden, who was one of the last surviving 1946 British Lions 'Indomitables' tourists. The opportunity to talk to Bryn was too important to miss and we spent a magical few hours with him and his

---

[1] Portelli, Allesandro, 'Memory and Resistance, For a History (and Celebration) of the Circolo Bosio' in *The Battle of Valle Giulia*. University of Wisconsin Press, 1997.

wife at their home in Blackpool listening to their memories of the tour and other events both in and away from rugby league during Bryn's fascinating career.

The extracts which have been chosen for inclusion are intended to provide a broad account of rugby league's rich history over the 90 or so years since Stanley Pickles could remember first visiting Headingley in 1915. This period has been punctuated by two World Wars, global depressions, the end of empire, the rise of multicultural society in Britain and the decline of industries upon which many communities across West Yorkshire were built. These events have had a profound impact on both rugby league and the communities in which the game is played and it is hoped that the transformation which has taken place is reflected in the pages of this book.

Six of the seven chapters have been divided into three chronological sections which represent key periods in the game's history. The first covers the period up to 1945 and aims to show how rugby league was shaped by the years of depression in the industrial north during the inter-war period as well as the various ways in which the game responded to the national crisis that followed the outbreak of the second global conflict. The second period covers the years from 1945 to 1970 when in common with most other spectator sports the end of the Second World War initially led to a boom period of large crowds and high interest in the game. But then, as Britain recovered from the ravages of war, rugby league began to fall into decline during the 1960s in the face of increasing competition from new forms of leisure which were created by the rise of consumer society. The last section covers the years from 1970 to 1995 during which further challenges were faced. Structural industries in the north reached a point of chronic decline and were dismantled in a way which severely affected many communities across the region as the British economy was remodelled during the 1980s.

Of the six chapters that make up the book five are based around themes which are common to any period of the game's history. The first is based upon the early memories of the people we interviewed and these recollections were often amongst the most vivid which were recalled in the interviews. Often they refer to events that shaped peoples subsequent relationships with the game, with bonds of family, friendship and community featuring strongly. For someone like Trevor Ward, whose father Ernest captained Bradford Northern and Great Britain in the 1940s and 1950s, rugby league was at the hub of life during his early years, while John Beaumont's passion for the game was ignited by hours spent as a child with family friend Hubert Pogson, a former Huddersfield player, at the club's famous old Fartown ground.

Throughout its history rugby league been such an important part of life in some West Yorkshire communities that it was almost impossible to not take an interest in the game. Harry Jepson, Alf Burnell and

Frank Watson all remember how rugby league provided a welcome distraction from the hardship of life during their formative years in Hunslet during the 1920s and 1930s. Alf and his friends used rolled up newspaper as a makeshift ball and Alan Bradford remembered blowing up a pig's bladder for the same purpose when he played rugby on the streets of Dewsbury as a child during the 1950s. Graham Chalkley's first memories on the other hand revolve around the celebrity of Sharlston's most famous rugby league family; the Foxes, who lived in the house next to his school playground.

Some people, however, had very different introduction to the game. Originally from Ireland, Donald Hunt took a farm in Featherstone after serving in the Army during the Second World War. His interest in rugby league was first aroused by the conversation of workers on the land he farmed which bordered onto the Post Office Road ground.

The game's links with local communities feature heavily throughout the book and fittingly provide the main focus for the second chapter. Along with association football and cricket, popular interest in rugby grew rapidly during the second half of the 19th century in towns and villages across West Yorkshire which had been transformed almost beyond recognition by a period of incredible urban industrial growth. Clubs were formed in almost every community and the game helped forge a sense of collective identity in a world that had changed fundamentally. In many cases this close relationship has since been maintained and offers a window into a whole range of broader issues and events. Bernard Shooman, for example, explained how interest in the game developed among the Jewish community in Leeds despite the difficulties they faced from the demands of their faith. Sid Rookes, Alf Burnell, Joe Warham and Bryn Knowelden, however, all recounted the different ways in which the Second World War shaped their lives as well as their rugby league careers.

The working lives of players who for much of the game's history combined full-time employment outside the game with a professional playing career also features strongly in this chapter. For fans such as Geoff Wright, mixing regularly in everyday life with some of the Halifax players he watched at Thrum Hall forged a special bond which for him and many others helped define the game's distinctive character.

A variety of different perspectives on the often difficult task of managing a rugby league club is also provided in this chapter. Doris Beard remembers what life was like as the first woman to be employed as secretary of a rugby league club in the 1950s. Ronnie Wolfenden, on the other hand, recounts some of the frustrations he encountered trying to find new sources of revenue and change the outlook of his fellow Halifax directors when crowds began to dwindle during the 1960s and 1970s.

The third chapter examines the experience of playing rugby league during a period in which different approaches were developed by players and coaches as the game changed significantly following a series of alterations to its rules. Players such as Frank Watson and Sid Rookes who grew up in the 1930s explain how through constantly playing rugby as children they developed skills which were translated into the instinctive attacking style that prevailed before the 1950s. The next two decades, however, saw the development of new approaches to coaching which resulted in a golden period of international dominance for the English game. John Atkinson remembers how his career was influenced during this period by the pioneering methods of Roy Francis. In the 1970s and 1980s rugby league coaching methods continued to progress and Maurice Bamford and Peter Fox, two hugely successful figures throughout these years, give an insight into their approach to the game prior to rugby league's modern era.

The specialisation of playing roles is another thread which runs through this chapter. In particular some of the techniques employed in the lost art of scrummaging are explained by Frank Wagstaff and Keith Bridges who as field side prop and hooker often tested the rules to win possession of the ball which was so pivotal to the outcome of games before the 1990s. As more opportunities were available to compete for possession during the era of contested scrums, ball-playing half-backs were often encouraged to express their skills to the full. Bak Diabira gives an insight into how he attempted to open up the defensive line when it was positioned just five yards from the play the ball.

But as well as recalling how these high level skills made the game so appealing to play and watch Bak and other former players such as Maurice Bamford also provide a graphic illustration of rugby league's brutality during this period when for many violence was an accepted part of the game. The important role played by amateur rugby league as a form of recreation and a route into the professional game is also featured in the chapter.

The fourth chapter offers the perspective of those who have watched and refereed rugby league over the past nine decades. Stanley Pickles's fascinating and remarkably lucid accounts of the matches he saw during the inter war period show that fans back then were gripped by the same incident packed excitement and intense rivalries that are offered by the game today. The memories of Maurice Bamford, Keith Bell, John Beaumont, Paul Kilbride and others also emphasise this thread of continuity by showing how the adventure of travelling to away matches or Wembley cup finals elicited a sense of excitement and anticipation among fans during any era.

Different aspects of crowd behaviour and fan culture are other facets of the game which left a strong mark in the memories of supporters such as Geoff Wright and Paul Kilbride while Geoff Smith and Andy Coldrick illustrate the strong sense of loyalty many fans feel towards their local clubs. In contrast to events on the pitch, accounts of violence among spectators were almost nonexistent in the interviews we carried out during the project. However, Geoff Wright's recollections of how the brutality he saw among players was encouraged by fans provides a further illustration of the culture of violence which existed on the field for much of the game's history.

The memories of those who have officiated rugby league matches at both amateur and professional level also provide a unique and fascinating view of the game. Billy Thompson recounts his experiences with the characteristic blend of humour, honesty and thought-provoking insight which lay at the heart of his success as a leading referee. He explains how it felt to be the only man on the field who had no one on his side. Although he also officiated in professional rugby league, Bernard Shooman's career as a referee was mostly spent in the amateur game. He remembers that this could be a tough environment for match officials which at times exposed the unsavoury side of some communities where the game is played.

All sports are in some way defined by their leading personalities and major events and these themes provide the basis for the next two chapters. From pioneers of domestic and international rugby league to the famous players who graced each era of the game's history, rugby league has more than its share of legendry figures. Many early stars have become part of the mythology of the game through stories passed on from one generation to the next, especially amongst family members or the communities with which they were associated.

A number of former players also offer a unique perspective on personalities who they came into contact with on and off the field. Joe Warham outlines the attributes that made Brian Bevan the game's greatest ever try scorer, while Mick Morgan explains why Keith Bridges was arguably the world's leading hooker in the 1970s.

There are also stories of inspirational personalities who have left an indelible mark on the players whose paths they crossed. Bryn Knowelden gives a wonderfully warm account of the influence Tommy McCue had on him and other members of the famous 'Indomitables' 1946 touring party to Australia and New Zealand. Players such as Keith Bell, Bak Diabira and John Sheridan on the other hand explain how the knowledge and enthusiasm of coaches such as Tommy Smales, Albert Fearnley and Harry Street were a seminal influence on their careers.

Throughout its history the game has also been shaped by a number of key administrators at clubs and the Rugby Football League itself. One of the most influential – and sometimes controversial – was Bill Fallowfield. As secretary of the RFL he effectively ran the game between 1945 and 1974. He is remembered by Eddie Bottomley, the RFL's assistant secretary for much of that time. Derek Hallas, on the other hand, recalls the friendship he had with club chairman John Smallwood during his playing days at Keighley.

Major domestic and international matches have also had a profound impact upon rugby league and the extreme contrast between success and failure on these great occasions has aroused the passions of both fans and players to create a wealth of momentous events.

Wembley, of course, holds a special place in the culture of rugby league and this is reflected throughout the chapter. Fans recount a variety of memories from Morris and Harry Child's initial scepticism about whether the final should have been moved to the capital in 1929 to Linda Kitson's recollections of various trips to Wembley in the 1980s and a memorable encounter with some of the Wigan stars of that period. Graham Chalkley provides a unique eye witness perspective on aftermath of the 1968 Challenge Cup Final and its impact upon the great Don Fox. Ken Dean, however, recounts how the anti-climax of playing in a drawn Wembley Cup Final was followed by the unforgettable experience of an iconic event, the 1954 Odsal replay.

Rugby league's greatest stage has, however, arguably been provided by international football. Since the first party set sail in 1910 most British players consider the pinnacle of a career in the game to be selection for a Lions tour to the southern hemisphere. Many of these epic ventures have also become part of the rugby league folklore and Bryn Knowelden recalls his experiences on one of the most historic, the 'Indomitables' tour of 1946. But a more notorious occasion is remembered by Mick Morgan who played in the brutal England against Wales World Cup contest at Lang Park Brisbane in 1975.

The final chapter takes a different format from the previous six by focusing solely upon the game in the modern era. The intention here is to provide a broad view of how those involved in rugby league now see the revolutionary changes which took place in the sport during the 1990s as well as subsequent developments which have helped the game adapt to the changing social and economic landscape of the 21st century. Understandably the advent of Super League features strongly and reactions to the initial proposals along with their planned mergers are recounted by David Hinchcliffe and Gerry Wright. David also provides a fascinating insight into the prelude to the momentous events which changed both codes of rugby in 1995 through memories of his role in the All-Party Parliamentary Rugby League Group.

Some clubs took immediately to the brash new world of Super League and at Bradford existing supporters such as John Downes as well as newcomers to the game like Gill Johnson remember how the early success of the Bulls characterised an era of excitement and entertainment at Odsal. Francis Stephenson on the other hand provides a player's perspective on life as a full-time professional in the game's new 'promised land'.

There was, of course, another side to the advent of Super League and a very different set of circumstances was faced by Bramley, one of the clubs which seemed to be overlooked in the new scheme of things.

Andy Coldrick recounts how the absolute despair he and other fans felt as the club folded in 1999 was eventually followed by an incredible sense of euphoria when five years of hard work by a group of dedicated supporters led to its resurrection.

The last four decades have also seen the impact of changing attitudes to broader social issues and a growing culture of regulation reach across all sports. The introduction of initiatives to improve equity and diversity in rugby league as well as the health, safety and welfare of players and supporters has led to a number of welcome developments. Paul Kilbride remembers the incredible support he received from throughout the game after a tragic accident suffered while playing left him paralysed. He has since become involved with the Rugby League Benevolent Fund which was later set up to provide support for players who have suffered serious injuries.

Richard and Gill Johnson remember how they were involved in the formation of the Rugby League Disabled Supporters Association in 2005 to improve facilities and help rugby league grounds comply with the Disability Discrimination Act.

While rugby league has a proud record of embracing players from different ethnic backgrounds, the game is not free from discriminatory attitudes which exist in wider society. Both Ikram Butt with the British Asian Rugby Association and Stan Timmins through his studies at Leeds Metropolitan University talk about the work they have done to help identify and address the reasons for rugby league's failure to attract substantial interest amongst many ethnic minority communities.

The chapter also includes some wise words from Gerry Wright, one of numerous people who campaigned against the proposed mergers which alarmed many when the introduction of Super League was announced in 1995. Looking back on the way the game has developed since then, he sums up a common feeling among rugby league supporters that the changes have generally been for the good and helped give the game a wider appeal which has enabled it to adapt to the new context of sport in the age of mass media, satellite television and globalisation. But, like David Hinchliffe, he recognises that the relationship with the game's traditional communities over the last 115 years remains at the heart of British rugby league and must be preserved to ensure a healthy future.
Robert Light

Editing
Michael O'Hare did his usual thorough job sub-editing the original draft of this book. However, to retain authenticity, we kept sub-editing changes to a minimum and thus did not use much of his work. We have used footnotes on occasions to clarify anything that was unclear and correct occasional lapses of memory.

Contents

Remembering Sharlston Colliery. Rugby league had strong links with coal mining from the sport's earliest days. (Photo: Peter Lush)

Yorkshire versus Lancashire at Huddersfield 18 October 1950: Back: Arthur Wilmot (Huddersfield), Bernard Poole (Leeds), Bill Metcalfe (Hunslet), Jim Bowden (Huddersfield), Jim Booth (Wakefield T), John Etty (Batley), Ken Traill (Bradford N); front: Alf Burnell (Hunslet), Arthur Wood (Featherstone R), Dick Cracknell (Huddersfield), Ernest Ward (Bradford N, capt.), Ken Dean (Halifax), Stan Thompson (Dewsbury). (Courtesy *Rugby League Journal*)

Cumberland versus Yorkshire at Workington 7 September 1966. The match was a 17–17 draw. (Courtesy Robert Gate)

1. Discovering the game

Before 1945

Sitting on the straw

It started when my mam said "For goodness sake take him up", she said, "Give me a bit of peace", and he took me.

I was only four years old. He took me to Headingley and I remember it to this day, going through the turnstiles and the click, click, click of them underneath me. I was on my dad's shoulder.

There was straw on the field in them days and I was on the straw. I don't know who they were playing, but I watched the match and it was the first time I'd been. It would be about 1915, I was born in 1911.

Stanley Pickles

Ordinary working men

I was born in Hunslet in a back-to-back house and my uncle took me to Parkside. He used to watch Hunslet, he was a member. His season ticket cost him 25 shillings, for that he had a centre stand seat for first and second team rugby. He watched the cricket and as a member of the board he could use the pavilion.

He took me to this match, it was Hunslet versus Featherstone Rovers and I think it was the first game Jack Walkington, who was a great servant for Hunslet, played. I didn't know anything about it. Hunslet played in white in those days and I suddenly realised that … the Hunslet team performing these wonderful feats of athleticism on the field, I used to see them when they were going to work. I lived in my grandmother's house and I couldn't believe it was the same people.

I remember the week after [my first match] – I didn't live with my grandmother then – but I used to go for the weekend, I remember seeing players like, in this particular instance, Jim Bacon who played for Leeds. But there were scores of Hunslet players who worked in the factories. The place was full of factories. I thought "that was the same chap I saw on Saturday afternoon." I couldn't believe that on Saturday afternoon, ordinary working men who wore overalls going down the street were transformed into giants on the rugby field and I was hooked. I don't think I've ever lost that feeling now.

One of the great things about rugby league is that the stars of the game, whether they are in Australia, New Zealand or anywhere, are still ordinary human beings. They'll talk to you to about everyday things, which is very different from some of the major sports stars of today who live in a completely different world. At Headingley one of the great things, and it applies to all clubs of course, is that after the match players come and mingle with the supporters. It has always

1

been the same you know, they've never lost the common touch no matter how great. Take someone like Roger Millward, he at times is humble and what a great player he was. So that is what attracted me to the game and I became a fervent Hunslet supporter.

That was in 1927. I'd seen a rugby game before that, I don't know much about it, it was at Wakefield. My uncle took me because he said "I want you to see the 'Prince of Centres', that was [Harold] Wagstaff." He played in a benefit game, I can't remember anything about it really but I do remember he took me.

Of course Wagstaff was regarded as the greatest of all time at that time. I'd be about five or six. He captained the 1914 [Great Britain] team and 1920 team and then [Jonty] Parkin became the captain in 1924. So I can't remember much about that game but I do remember I saw Harold Wagstaff play.
Harry Jepson

Lou Brown and Fred Adams
I became interested in rugby league and in Halifax because I lived in Triangle which is four miles out of Halifax, and started watching them from 10 years of age. I was 10 when they played in the third Wembley Rugby League Cup Final against York and that was the 1930–31 season.

I remember the very first one, 1928–29 with Dewsbury and Wigan and the gate then was 41,500. When Halifax played York it was 40,368. Halifax won 22-8.

It was a remarkable final that. I didn't see it, I was only a laddie of 10 you see and my father wasn't particularly interested in rugby league, so I didn't go to Wembley. But I listened to it on the radio. At the time Halifax had a marvellous wing threequarter called Lou Brown, a New Zealand All-Black rugby union player who they signed.

He pretty well got them to Wembley. He scored the vital tries in the previous rounds. In fact in the semi-final that year they played St Helens at Rochdale, on the Rochdale [rugby league] ground which was quite a good ground in those days. They play on the soccer ground at Rochdale today.

There was a gate then of getting on for 40,000 [and] the spectators overspilled onto the ground. There were a number of policemen on horseback and, it was always said, Lou Brown got the winning try underneath the stomach of a police horse.

I forget what the score was, but there was only one try scored and he scored it and it was supposed to be remarkable. I think that was the first season he played for Halifax, but unfortunately he didn't play in the final. It was a tragedy really because the week leading up to the final – he was a bit of a lad – he'd gone off on a drinking session apparently and they didn't know where he had gone to. They lost him.

2

He didn't turn up for training, so although he was such an outstanding player they actually dropped him, left him out of the Wembley side.

I remember as a boy I was sick because he wasn't going to be playing and everybody saying 'no chance without Lou Brown'. Anyhow they played a local lad in his place called Fred Adams. He was born and bred in Halifax. I played cricket with his brother at Triangle a number of years ago. This Fred Adams, who was a second team wing threequarter, was the hero and man-of-the-match. He scored a try and kicked four goals. In those days a try was three points and a goal two points, so he got 11 of the 22 points. He became a hero when Halifax won the cup.

Ronnie Wolfenden

Rugby league and my existence

My dad was a keen sports fan particularly rugby league, football and boxing. When Keighley got to Wembley, Keighley were the local team, he lived in Skipton nine miles down the road. He'd been to Wembley an odd time before that but obviously when Keighley got to Wembley he wasn't going to miss out. In fact all the family went; my granddad who I hardly knew, his brother, a cousin, a second cousin, you name it; the whole clan went out of my dad's side of the family.

My mother had only just left school and started working, she'd heard of rugby, but didn't know the difference between league and union. She came from a devout church-going village, Gargrave, just four miles up the road from Skipton. With Keighley getting to Wembley there was [also] a special train trip to London to see the coronation decorations because it was the [King's] coronation the same week as Keighley were there, in 1937. They announced it in the church before she went that she was going to London.

So she'd gone with two or three of her friends who she'd just met at work to London on this special train trip to see the coronation decorations. My father and the gang had gone to see Keighley play at Wembley. For either of them going to London in those days, from humble working backgrounds, was the trip of a lifetime. So my father and the gang were having a look down at the sights in the morning before the match; they'd gone on one of the special trains from Keighley. Either one of my dad's clan or one of my mother's clan recognised the other as being from Skipton. So that's where they hit it off: down The Mall.

So all this talk about Johnny Wilkinson's famous drop-goal as being the most famous rugby score of all time, well regarding my existence and that of my brother, it was a guy called Lou Bevan who ran 40 yards in the Challenge Cup semi-final replay in 1937. If that hadn't have happened you wouldn't be talking to me right now. So I owe my very existence to rugby league.

Roger Ingham

Converted from soccer

Well I was a footballer really; I played football at school and after, when I was 14. I went with my mate [to rugby], with the local team, Kippax and they were a man short. They talked me into playing and somebody gave me a pair of pads, if I'd play.

I would be about 18, I was born in 1916, so 1934. We played Normanton, I remember that. I didn't know the rules or anything. I played at second-row and my mate said "follow me" so I followed him all the time. When they kicked off, somebody kicked ball and gave me a black eye. I said I'd never play no more. But I did.

I carried on with the local amateur team for about two seasons and then I went to Methley, because they paid us a bit of money, half a crown I think it was, and I used to go on the bike. So I made half a crown. They were in the Leeds League, a bit higher than our Castleford League. Only half a crown, but it was expenses. I worked down the pit all the time when I played.

I got to Hunslet from the *Yorkshire Evening Post*. They said bring your boots and you can have a game at the beginning of the season. And I went and I got signed on. I played in a few games in the 'A' team and then I got in the first team. They were a good side, [Billy] Thornton, Jack Walkington at full-back, Eddie Bennett, a very good team. In fact they'd just won the rugby league Cup the year before.
Frank Wagstaff

Scrambling for coppers

Well, when I was a child, I used to go down to the Rovers and it used to be comical because at half-time they left the football on the field. I was only about eight or nine years old and all the kids used to go on the field, picking the ball up and running, the others getting them down. But I didn't see many matches because we couldn't afford to go in, and it was only a penny.

I was born in 1922, so it would be about 1930 or 1931. That's how we used to follow the Rovers then. We used to wait until the end for the players coming out and if they'd got any coppers they used to throw them up in the air and the kids used to scramble for them.

But my mother and father followed Featherstone Rovers right from when they started. They were playing in a final at Swinton, or they were playing Swinton, and my dad had an old motor bike and he took my mother on the back. Coming back home it was raining and as you know the roads weren't tip top in those days. He went over a bump and he dropped her in a pool of water. He went two or three miles before he found out he'd lost her and had to go back!
Jackie Blackburn

A farmer's tale

It goes back to 1950, when I came to Featherstone as a farmer. We had a lot of casual labour at various times of the year and one of the people that came who was very interested in farming was Kenny Welburn, who was a prop forward for Featherstone.

When we were working, of course all the talk was about the team and the matches and everything else. I'd come from rugby union really and didn't know what this was all about. In 1952, at the start of the cup run, the first round was two legs and we played Rochdale. We just won the first leg away from home and the second one was at home. So I thought I'd go along and see this and really got hooked from then. Most unexpectedly we got to the final at Wembley in 1952 and got beaten by Workington Town. But it was a very good match and they showed up very well.

I'm from Ireland originally, went through the war, got badly wounded and was invalided out, then went farming in Featherstone, practically by the side of the Junction Hotel ... still is a famous pub. We farmed there for 15 years.

Practically all the income [in Featherstone] was from the mines, either working in the mines or shopkeepers or businesses that were connected with the mine – there was practically nothing else. I had two regular men and, for hay time, harvest time and potato time, we used to have gangs coming in. [The miners] worked shifts and if the shift was convenient, they'd come along and, of course, for the potato picking we got a lot of the wives and children. In fact the schools used to have a week off, I think it was the second week in October, so the kids would go and help with the potato picking.

They discussed the game the Saturday before and all the people who should be dropped and who they would pick for the following week. It was a real hotbed. I loved it, because I was always very keen on sport and I had a tremendous admiration for the club. I think I very quickly got embroiled in it myself and probably was as passionate as anybody.

Donald Hunt

Pigs' bladders in old cases

I started when Harry Smith and Laurie Gant ran a coaching course up at Thornhill field and they started us all off playing. Then the open age used to play touch-and-pass on a Sunday morning. So we started going down and they were like "you're not playing, you're not playing" so we played ourselves. Then the open age were right good to us and they let us join in.

Then I got right interested and I started going fetching sawdust and marking the field, me and a lad called Kenny Sykes. I'd be about 13 or 14. Then we got a side going, Thornhill side, and it didn't last long. But we started another one with Bernard Watson, Johnny Harpin,

Alan Wood, and they were very good.[2] Clarry Watson could see the potential and he took over, which was brilliant because he was a good fella and got the committee going. We got the gatehouse at the park and turned it into dressing rooms.

But it was brilliant, we all stuck together and worked hard. But like Cora [Haley] says [see above] we did it for the love of it, and it was something to do, we had nothing to do in those days. Sometimes we didn't have a rugby ball, so to play touch-and-pass in the park we used to roll old socks up into a ball just to make a rugby ball.

Many a time we used pigs' bladder inside old cases which we didn't have an inner tube for. We used the pig's bladder which used to be fairly strong, put them in, blow 'em up, tied a knot and put a lace into the ball, because you couldn't afford inner tube, they were dear. Only probably one lad had a rugby ball that we knew and we daren't go for him because his mother and dad didn't want him to laik rugby.

You lived for it. It sounds funny, but I couldn't wait for Saturday to have a game of rugby, I couldn't wait. It was the same at school. Anytime there was a game at school, I was there ready. In fact that's why I'm so thick, I blew the balls up all the time instead of doing my lessons.
Allan Bradford

Rumbling clogs and local heroes
My very first memories were before I even went to a match because we actually lived on Gibbet Street [Halifax]. When I was very tiny they used to play on a Saturday afternoon and we could hear the noise when the men left the match at Thrum Hall to walk down Gibbet Street towards town. I can remember being very, very tiny and me and my sister used to hear the noise, like a rumbling because most of them wore clogs. They used to go straight from work, as they used to work Saturday mornings then, and there was this noise of clogs and chattering and it got louder and louder as it came closer and closer. We used to run out to sit on the steps to watch them all go past to see if they had won or lost and just watch these waves of men just stream down from Thrum Hall. There were thousands and thousands of them walking down Gibbet Street all together as they left the match.

We never actually went to Thrum Hall when we were small because my dad was a footballer. He used to go down to the Shay and quite often he used to ask us if we wanted to come. We did do, but he never ever went to the rugby matches.

When I was about seven, we lived in a back-to-back house down Gibbet Street and one of the Halifax rugby players moved in behind for

---

[2] Watson turned professional with Leeds, Wood signed for Halifax and Harpin for Hunslet. Other pioneers of the club who turned professional included G. Haley with Bradford Northern, A. Cauthard and E. Hinchliffe for Dewsbury, J. Maloney with Hull and T. Hamshaw for Halifax. Many others also entered the professional game.

quite a while. Many of the children around about all used to gather together to watch him come home from work – he was a painter and decorator by trade. The thing that we found most unusual about him was that he had a different coloured skin to what we had, he was really black. He had come up from Wales, and we had actually never seen anybody that colour before. Hundreds of us used to pile out to watch him come home from work and watch him walk down the road.

His name was Johnny Freeman and it turned out that he was a really good, fast winger. Quite a number of us used to gather together and walk up to Thrum Hall to watch him play in the matches, but we never had any money to go in. About 10 minutes into the second half at Thrum Hall, they used to open the gates so all the children and OAPs and people that couldn't afford to pay in would go in to watch. We always used to ask Johnny to save all his tries for those last 20 minutes or so in the second half.

He always used to say "I'll remember when you're coming in and I'll score a few tries for you," but I don't think he did, he just used to score tries. That was the first time that I remember going to matches. It got me hooked onto rugby and I've been following Halifax ever since.

Linda Kitson

Getting back on my feet
My first memory is my first game. I started training at Dewsbury and I hadn't a clue, because I was a footballer. I played for Birstall Rovers before I went in the army. I was called up to the army and got in the army side. I had chance to go to professional football, but I didn't think I was good enough for football. I just think I lacked one or two things. I was fast enough and I could strike the ball as a forward pretty well. But I didn't think I was good enough.

So I decided to go and play rugby league for some money, because any national serviceman coming out of the Army, unless they came from a rich family, they were coming out, same as me, with nothing. I hadn't even a suit. I bought a suit for £1/10s off a Scots lad. I think three of us wore it in the army, and I had that for demob. So I decided that I wanted to earn money fast, as quickly as I could, to get some clothes together and get myself on my feet.

I met some friends that played. Brian Foley, who played with Dewsbury, took me to Dewsbury. Dewsbury wanted to sign me, but couldn't afford to at that time. Dewsbury were a poor side financially. I was advised to go to Batley where they were just slightly better off.

Batley, I really enjoyed. They made me welcome, they fitted me in nicely, they helped me out as being a beginner, never played amateur. But they knew I had a bit of ability, speed wise, sidestepping and I learned from Arthur Staniland, ex-Leeds and Castleford wingman and Frank Watson. Dave Valentine was a great coach. He looked after me,

he came just after. I was 21, which is old in some respects, because lads are playing at 16.
Eddie Illingworth

Television stars in a rugby mad village
I went to school in this rugby mad village, Sharlston. As probably a 10-year-old I was in the school playground and the famous Fox brothers lived in the caretaker's house. Tommy Fox and Stella Fox, they were the caretakers and Peter, Don and Neil lived in the caretaker's house.

I was in the playground and BBC TV cameras rolled up. *Sportsnight* it was in them days and I think it was on a Thursday night. So out of the house came Don and Neil. I think they were playing in some kind of final or a semi-final. Eddie Waring was there and the cameras started rolling: Don and Neil coming out of the house and the kids were in the playground. What they did was pick two sides to play touch-and-pass.

One went on Don's side and one went on Neil's side. I was very, very fortunate to be on Don's side and Eddie Waring was doing the commentating.
Graham Chalkley

'Right, we'll have a go!'
I was always keen on ball games as a kid. I used to play lots and lots and lots of table tennis. I used to play a fair bit of cricket, anything that involved a ball. I wouldn't say I was brilliant at everything that involved a ball, but I did better than most. But soccer, all I lived for was soccer, and then when we converted to become a rugby school I was heartbroken, absolutely heartbroken.

The first time we went to the playing fields with this new sports master who told us, 11-year-old kids "You're going to become a rugby playing school and you're never going to play soccer again." I thought "What's all this about?" You should have a choice, you shouldn't have things forced on you and this was forced on us. It was "You either play this or you don't play anything."

But me and my mates said "Right we'll have a go," and fortunately we were pretty good at it. Then they formed a side, they made me captain and I thought "Well, let's have a go" and I never looked back, things got better and better and better.

This is one of the strangest things: as a schoolboy playing school rugby from the age of 11 till the day I left school, I never played at scrum-half. I never played a match at scrum-half for my school side. It was only when I represented Hull schoolboys that I played scrum-half.

I played at left centre, because I had the number 4 shirt and that was always my favourite number, which it still is. They picked another lad to play at scrum-half who was as good as anybody at that position I suppose. They said to me "You're a left centre" and I said "What

12

does a left centre do?" They said "You get your winger in for tries and look after your winger." So I thought "fair enough" and that was it.

I just read, I read all the time. I acquired a rule book from the headmaster of the school. The headmaster I had, I can't pay him a high enough compliment, because without him I don't think I'd have reached the standard of anything in life. Harry Foster, he's dead now and I had so much admiration for this guy, he helped me tremendously. The area I was brought up in Hull, a lot of guys went wrong and I could have gone wrong as well, but this guy, I had so much respect for him, I thought "No, I'll do what he wants me to do."

I used to just read and read and read and got the rule book. I remember as a 12-year-old I'd be playing, and the schools referees were teachers, and they'd be blowing their whistle. I'd be putting them to task and saying "Oh no, I'm sorry sir," always address them correctly, "I'm sorry, you're wrong sir." I remember one game vividly where a young guy was terrified of being tackled and threw the ball straight into touch. The referee blew, scrum down and I said "No sir, no. It's a penalty to us because you can't do that." That was the rule, I don't know whether it still is now. But the ruling was if you throw the ball directly into touch it's a penalty to the opposing side. That's how I was, always controversial, but there you go.

Bak Diabira

Miss Collinson
It's a kind of gradual memory with rugby league for me. I'm from Hunslet, which is obviously a strong rugby league area and I went to Hunslet Carr School. Now, in my younger years I didn't really take to rugby league. I wasn't really bothered about it.

I was aware that Hunslet was a strong team. Hunslet used to come into the school at the start of each season with season-ticket offers, which I never took up, and one big regret I've got is that, at the time I was at Hunslet Carr, the teacher who took the rugby league team, which was always strong, left. They didn't have another teacher to take over and the teacher who stepped forward to actually run the rugby league team was a lady, Miss Collinson.

That was a fantastic big story at the time. Now it's not really unusual for a woman to be involved in rugby league. But Miss Collinson took the team over and at the time *Grandstand* had a kind of starting credit where it revolved around the old style cameras which had four lenses and each lens had a shot of something. One may have been the Grand National, another may have been the FA Cup Final and one of them was a shot of Miss Collinson tackling Jack Haigh who was a roly-poly prop we had. So that was a big thing which I actually missed out on.

I passed my 11-plus and went to the Central High School in Leeds, which was a soccer-playing school. I didn't know anything about

soccer either, because soccer was a complete alien game in south Leeds at the time. You didn't see a Leeds United scarf or anybody playing soccer. This was in 1963 and I popped round one Saturday lunchtime to call on my pal Graham Lister – Lizer – to play out. It must have been about one o' clock in the afternoon and I got round to his house and he's just climbing in his dad's van. I said "Where are you going Lizer?" He said "I'm off down to Parkside" and his dad said to me "Run home and get a tanner, Oggy, and come back and we'll take you down". So I ran back and I got sixpence and here we are now, 49 years on, completely engrossed in rugby league.
Phil Hodgson

Being up close

My dad took me to McLaren Field to see Bramley versus Blackpool on 15 April 1968, I know that Bramley won, but I can't remember the score. My abiding memory was the crowd was right up against the touchline so you could touch the players. One memory did stick with me from that time. Although Bramley won the game fairly comfortably, a Blackpool guy went over the try line to score, but before he touched the ball down the defence elbowed him into touch and he went into the barriers where the supporters were and didn't score.

I just remember as a nine-year-old at the time, thinking what a fantastic game this is, full of collisions, excitement, ball-handling and lots of different skills. So I was hooked from that day and we actually went back the following day because Bramley played Wakefield Trinity. I can't remember the score, the memory is less vivid from that day. But it was just being up close from such an early age. It seemed an exciting sport to watch and to play as well. But definitely that was a vivid memory from Blackpool in my first game.

I left primary school and went to secondary school at Abbey Grange in Leeds, we played rugby league there. I went to school with Kevin Dick, who played for Leeds rugby league and in the year below me was Peter Lister, who played for Bramley for a number of years and is now leading try scorer. There was big sense of everybody playing rugby league. It was football or rugby league basically and we had lots of people at school who were very good at both and went on and pursued careers in either code.
Andy Coldrick

1970 to 1995

Choosing sirloin steak

I arrived in England on 7 December 1970 at Heathrow and the chairman of Wakefield Trinity, Les Pounder and his secretary were waiting. They had a board and the board said "Are you Dave Barends?" I'd been negotiating with them and a legal representative in

Cape Town, Jim Windsor, who was the guy who initially brought me to England. I'd been negotiating with these people for a period of time and when I came to England that's what I saw.

At that point I went with the flow because I suddenly realised that people may not be aware that I do speak English and well, but [as a] second language of course. I introduced myself and then we caught the train to Wakefield. Coming from South Africa, very hot, it was like being put into a freezer and I was thinking, if I have to play in that, "What am I doing?"

From there we travelled north and I remember the chairman saying to the secretary Eddie Thomas "Have we got enough money, I wonder what he wants to eat?" So we were sitting in the compartment travelling north on my journey. The cold, when I saw the white frost, I was prepared because I was told by people I'd contacted in South Africa who'd played rugby league in England [about] the weather and the difficulties that may be when I arrived.

When my chairman said "Do we have enough money?" I thought, well, "Are they for real?" But that explained rugby league to me because I did not know the background of rugby league and of course people have to manage. I realised that it was the beginning of something and you've got to run with it. They looked at the menu and said "I hope he doesn't pick sirloin steak". So of course I was going to pick sirloin steak and I just pointed at that. I realised these guys were playing a silly game, I'll play the same. They said "If he has a steak we'll have to have a sandwich," and I thought that'll do me.

When I arrived there was one person, she was a student, greeted me in English at Wakefield station. They were astonished, the two guys that I'd just travelled with, because they couldn't hold a conversation with me. So that explained rugby league to me.

David Barends

The photo is David Barends wearing the tie and blazer he was awarded as an 'Honorary Springbok'. This was given to players who were unable to play for South Africa during the apartheid era. (Photo: Peter Lush)

'Poggy' and his mates

My earliest memories are basically spending all my time at Fartown when I was a kid. I used to abscond from school to go, I spent hours and hours and hours driving round on the grass cutting machine. Ernie Scruper was a groundsman there. My father's best friend was a fellow called Hubert Pogson, he acted more like a grandfather to me, he was 60s or 70s or 80s as I was growing up. 'Poggy' as everybody knew him played for Fartown in the 1920 Northern Union Challenge Cup Final. Of course he knew all the old players, the famous people, like Ben Gronow. Harold Wagstaff, the greatest rugby league player of all time was his centre; he could look after himself on a rugby field and he looked after his wingers.

In the last season before the First World War broke out they won all four cups and of course the war broke out and rugby league was stopped. Basically they just picked up again after the war finished and football started again. They won the Yorkshire Cup, the Challenge Cup and they got to the Championship Final [in 1920] where they lost 3–2 to Hull. The man that scored the try for Hull was a man called Billy Batten, another famous player, and Poggy will swear blind he put his foot in touch before he scored the try; so they should have won all four cups yet again.

Poggy introduced me to these players, 40 or 50 years after they played, but they were gods. The man that at the time broke the goalkicking record in a season was Ben Gronow who came from Wales. He goes down in history as the first man to kick off at Twickenham rugby union [ground], I think he played for Wales against England, probably 1908 and he kicked off. So he broke the goalkicking record, most goals in a season and held the number of points [record] until Jim Sullivan came along. He taught me how to kick goals on the cricket field. The old leather football with laces, make sure it's stood straight up and laces are pointed down wind. That was the type of person that taught me.

Poggy's best friend was a fellow called Jack Armstrong who is notorious in rugby league for being a referee. He swore literally every other word. It didn't matter who you were, I always remember the Lord Mayor being at Fartown one day and he got the same treatment from Jack Armstrong as everybody else did. He was a referee so you can imagine the players try and stand up to this guy, he wouldn't take any notice, that was Poggy's best friend. When the weather got too bad we played dominoes in the club rather than being out on the field. So, as a kid, that was what I was brought up with.

I used to go to matches. I'm told the first time I ever went I was about 10 months old and I cried my eyes out because I was in the stand and the echo with the wooden stand. As I grew up I used to sit next to Poggy, now I had to sit next to Poggy because nobody else would. Every tackle that went in on the field, Poggy joined in. What

16

you used to find was everybody got knocked further along the bench because Poggy was digging his shoulder and they used to sit me next to him because I used to be able to get up quicker than everybody else.

That took me through to eight or nine or 10 years old. My dad died when I was 8 years old so I dropped off, I didn't go as much. But when I went to high school they were looking for volunteers for the school rugby league team. My hand shot up, you used to get free tickets as a schoolboy to get into the [Huddersfield] match. They used to play during the main match at half-time, the schoolboys were allowed to play in a competition. You played five minutes each way and I still have the bag with the dirt off my boots that I played in from the very first match.

I remember playing in a match, it's a massive field when you're only 11 years old, and I remember running the massive distance of about 25 yards to score a try. You weren't allowed to kick goals because nobody could kick it that high at that age. The crowd cheering, I thought it was absolutely wonderful. You went in the bath afterwards, a big proper bath, not silly old showers, and of course you were allowed to watch the match afterwards.

So I got hooked and started watching them all the time. I used to have to pay my money every week. Someone found out it was cheaper to buy a season ticket. But as an 11-year-old, one parent family, money wasn't great and my mother could never afford it. That was my job during the summer, find any job I could do to save enough money and one of my proudest moments – I think I was 12 or 13 – I went out and bought my own season ticket. It cost something like £8 for the season, but it was mine.

I still didn't go to school as often as I should have done, because I spent a lot of time at Fartown during the school days and because of that reason I got sent to a school in Hull: Trinity House. But I came home every weekend because I wanted to watch Fartown; that was the only reason. They used to kick off at half past three, which meant the match finished at five o'clock and the train left at 27 minutes past five.

I always lived no more than 10 minutes away from the ground, so I used to rush home pick my bag up and run down to the train station and catch the train back to Hull. The unfortunate thing at that time was that Hull and Hull Kingston Rovers especially were top of the rugby league and Huddersfield weren't, they were very close to the bottom. The amount of stick I got in Hull because I refused to deny that I was a Huddersfield fan.

John Beaumont

Keeping warm

When I started at high school, 11 years old, I'd never been interested in [rugby league] before. You had to do it for PE and I just got into it from there. That was Batley High School. Occasionally I'd been up [to watch Batley], but not right often. I don't know why, I just didn't bother and then I went to high school and started from there.

We had a team at school. I played with Roy Powell. He went to the same school. We were more or less in the same team. But then it changed to rugby union, which was alright. We got a new headmaster and he came from a rugby union background. So he changed things. It wasn't as good as rugby league, although I played for Yorkshire and England schools at rugby union. They were posh boys and me and Roy and Howard Bailey, being Batley lads, not being posh, they all went to grammar schools, they all seemed to fit in and we were like outcasts. That's how I looked at it anyway.

I did alright on the field, when I got the ball. I played on the wing and in those days they didn't seem to pass it to the wingers. It was kick and you had to run for it, that's how I got the ball. In rugby league your coaches always told you to come in looking for the ball and that's what I used to do. With having that bit of pace, you used to catch defences out going from acting half-back or coming infield. Sometimes when you were playing for school teams it was Saturday morning and absolutely freezing. So you didn't want to be stood on that wing, you wanted to keep warm and that's what you did, go in and get the ball as much as you could.

I didn't start with amateurs until I was 16. Because the last few years were rugby union, I wasn't interested once I'd left school. Then somebody asked me if I wanted to go up to Batley Boys and I went from there.

Carl Gibson

Television with Eddie Waring

I watched TV with Eddie Waring – the old black-and-white footage – watching the early Challenge Cup Finals. But my first memories of actually playing, I was brought up in Drighlington and was going to Morley Grammar school. We found out that the major sport was rugby union.

So I had to find out how to play rugby. Drighlington junior amateur [rugby league] club had just been set up at the time and we went there wanting to play rugby. We didn't know there were two codes of rugby at that time. Morley Grammar School was obviously a rugby union school and Drighlington junior amateur club was rugby league. So that was it really, we went there just because we were going to play rugby at school.

Karl Harrison

Playing in the streets

When I think back I must admit my first memory is playing rugby within our local streets, literally a stone's throw from Headingley. My brother Tony, his real name is Chris but he's known as Tony Butt, he's two years older than me and he started playing rugby at school. My dad bought him a rugby ball and we used to mess about in the streets. I've got three other brothers, and friends in our street used to get together. We were playing on the street, which was solid rock hard. But as kids that didn't bother us. We used to fall, graze our knees, get up and continue playing again.

So that's probably the earliest memories that I have; then obviously from the backyard streets into the school. Again, playing rugby in the school yard where it was just concrete, nobody seemed to mind, people getting hurt. We were young, about eight or nine. When we got really hurt we used to cry a few tears but once we recovered we were back in the game and getting involved.

My primary school was Brownhill School and that's where it all started. [I went to] middle school then, there was no secondary [School]. It was called Royal Park School, which is quite famous in regard to rugby players [who like] Norman Francis, for example, played for Leeds City boys and then signed for Leeds. He was quite a famous black rugby league player, one of my heroes. My brother, again, in his era, there was, Errol Johnson, Tony Butt, who played for Leeds City boys then went on to play for Leeds rugby league. So we had quite a few individuals who progressed extremely well.

There wasn't a team in the primary school but we still played it in the sports sessions. My brother was two years older than me and they had a rugby league team. But when I came to middle school they were looking to form a football team. They were encouraging us to play football and I said "I'm not that keen I want to play rugby". But they said "we don't actually have a rugby league team." So I had no choice but to play football. I enjoyed football. At one particular stage I actually thought I was going to be a football player because I played in the same team as David Batty, under-15 Leeds schoolboys. So it was a decent level, there were about seven, eight lads in that team who played for Yorkshire and a couple played for England. So it was quite a tough nut to crack. But I got an injury. I fractured my foot and by the time I came back, after a good couple of months out, the skill and fitness of the football players; they had gained so much advantage it was difficult to catch up. I was still playing rugby at the time, that was more natural to me and I could still keep up with the boys and so I took a diversion in regard to where I wanted to go.

I was very fortunate. When I was about 11, I represented Leeds City boys. We did quite well, we had a good team and we played a curtain raiser at St Helens before a Leeds – St Helens match. That's another wonderful occasion to remember. My dad, he passed away when I was 11. But he came to watch most of my games, if not all. He was there that time and we beat Saints.

I used to go to Headingley regularly to watch the games. I never paid because I never had any money, but at half-time they used to let us in. I remember people like John Holmes, John Atkinson, Dave Ward, Kevin Dick. These were people that stuck in my mind, heroes. When I eventually signed for Leeds as a 17-year-old to see all these players was like my dream come true, these were my heroes.

Ikram Butt

Giving it a go

My first memories of rugby league are watching it on the telly through the 1970s, the old Eddie Waring bandwagon, as such. I wasn't really interested in the game because I was a rugby union player. I was in the Royal Navy and based down in Portsmouth at various establishments in ships. So I just used to watch it on a Saturday afternoon in all its blood guts and glory, in the mud.

Then in 1977 I went fire fighting at Weeton barracks near Blackpool because the firemen went on strike, and a friend of mine arranged for me to have trial with Widnes. I said "Yeah, I'll give it a go". My position in rugby union was 11 [wing], so they said it's five or whatever and I had to get a book to find out what position five was and luckily enough it was a wing position.

So I went for a trial with Widnes. I wasn't successful, but Wakefield Trinity scouts were there and they asked me to go for trials, which I did. I think the first game was against Dewsbury, I scored two tries and they signed me on after that. The chairman wrote to the Navy and asked if I could be released in 1978. They released me and I went part-time rugby league then, because there was no full-time professionalism.

I was playing for the navy [at rugby union] and I'd played a couple of games for Cornwall. But at that time rugby union wasn't in leagues like it is today: they had diary fixtures. I also played for United Services, Portsmouth. They played teams like Harlequins, London Scottish, London Irish, Wasps and so on and so forth. But unfortunately, when fire fighting came in 1977 it stripped the United Services, Portsmouth team of a lot of its players. The first game was against Harlequins and they ran 73 points in unanswered, because it was more or less a third or fourth team. So because of that, through the course of that season, they lost all their good fixtures.

Stan Timmins

Getting on *Scrumdown*

I absolutely detested rugby league. I lived around the corner from a mate who was two years older and he played at a club called Otley Zebras rugby union. But they were always going to watch Leeds on a

Sunday and the first game I've got memories of was the Challenge Cup semi-final replay when Leeds got beat by Hull KR. We went because my dad went with my friend's dad. All I remember is being in what was the Kop at Elland Road and not really being able to see a thing. It didn't put me off, but I was always into football. Football was what everybody played.

Through another friend we started going on a Sunday down to Headingley. It was around 1988 and we use to go down at like quarter past one for a three o'clock kick off. The two dads would go to the bar and we'd go sit on the wall behind the goals opposite the old scoreboard end. We'd be sat there for about an hour and a half absolutely bored witless waiting for the game and it was the time before they put the seats in at the front of the North Stand. So what we decided after a few games was, because we were getting there so early we'd go into that little bit where I think it cost 50p and sit on the wall next to the [coaches'] benches and try and get on *Scrumdown*.

It was like if we were getting there so early we might as well sit in the best place we can and it was brilliant. You'd go the week after and be in the same place. But you'd have the [match] programme from two weeks before or what ever and might see yourself in the programme or you'd been on *Scrumdown*. They're sort of the earliest memories I've got of going to the games and after that I got right into it. After that first season we went to the away games as well and for about four or five seasons I didn't miss a game.

Paul Kilbride

Hunslet versus Warrington at Parkside around 1947.
Referee George Phillips awards a try. (Courtesy Robert Gate)

THE RAILWAY HOTEL

Following shootings
at the nearby colliery in 1893,
an inquest was held at this
public house.
In 1902 the famous
Featherstone Rovers R.L.F.C.
was formed here.

Rugby league has deep roots in Featherstone.
(Photo: Peter Lush)

2. Work and community life

Legends of the Leylands
There was a guy who many years ago did a series of articles called "Legends of the Leylands" in the *Jewish Gazette*. The story that was told, of course, was that the Jewish population in those days were in a sort of ghetto in the Leylands[3]. Invariably on their way home from the synagogue on a Saturday they used to go and watch Leeds Parish Church play, because the ground was very close to the Leylands, and being Saturday they wouldn't be carrying money[4]. The teams used to be very upset when they went round with the collection and nobody put any money in, and that was quoted as one of the reasons that Leeds Parish Church in their infinite wisdom decided to relocate to Cardigan Fields and then to Headingley.
Bernard Shooman

Tripe and onions
You had to work the week you played, or else you couldn't play. They had enough from playing at that time because a tradesman in them days, was it £3.50 a week they got? You know plumbers, electricians and such as that up to the war starting. That's when the wages started to shoot up they got £5 for a win and £4 and £3. So they were fairly well off if they were working an' all. They did all sorts of different jobs. My father, one of the directors found him a job and that was weaving at a place at Marsh. We lived in Elland and he brought one or two Welsh players to have suppers with us when they'd finished training and there were one or two Australians came.

Now this is funny. We used to like tripe and onions for us supper. Have you ever had any? By gum, you haven't lived have you? We had tripe and onions and this here Australian says, "That was nice Mrs Halliday. What was it?" My mother says to him "Tripe and onions". "What's that?" When she told him it was a cow's guts he just shot up stairs to be sick.
Fred Halliday

Hero worship in Hunslet
This hero worship that I was telling you about when I first went [to rugby matches], when I got a scholarship, I had to travel on the tram from the Middleton Estate down to the Grammar School in Hunslet at Cockburn. Some players lived at Middleton and one of them especially

---

[3] The Leylands was the main Jewish area in Leeds.
[4] Religious Jews would not carry money on the Sabbath as this could be construed as working, according to their religious beliefs.

got on the tram the stop before I got on and I knew which tram he got on: the ten past eight.

So I made sure that I got on that tram and he always sat, you won't remember, at the top of the tram steps. You came up the tram steps and Billy, he was a scrum-half, great player, he always sat at the top there and sometimes there was nobody sitting next to him. So I sat next to him and I was on the tram for about 10 minutes, quarter of an hour. I was plucking up courage to speak to him and before we got off, probably just passing Parkside, I'd say "It was a good game on Saturday, Billy" and he'd say "Yes, it was. We should have won" or something. So I got off the tram and went to school. "I've just been talking to Billy Thornton about last Saturday's game". Hero worship, it was wonderful because it was accessible. You see, it wasn't hero worship from afar. Billy went to his work at the Co-op Brush Works and he was a white collar worker.

Harry Jepson

Charlie Holmes's blacksmith's forge

My own involvement in rugby, I played as an amateur before the war as a young lad of 17 or 18 and I played for Luddenfoot in the local Halifax League. When I look back it was incredible really what we put up with. I lived at Triangle at the time and we used to get the bus or even walk to Luddenfoot over the tops via Sowerby and down to Luddenfoot. We stripped in a local forge, it was known as Charlie Holmes's blacksmith's forge, a mucky old place. We stripped in there and then we had about half-a-mile to walk to the ground up the hill, before we started playing and when you'd finished, of course, and you were caped in wet mud, you not only had to walk back, your legs were almost dropping off you. You walked back and there in Charlie Holmes' forge there was a couple of buckets of cold water and that's all you had, no showers or anything.

It just shows how things have changed because all the amateur rugby clubs, soccer clubs and cricket clubs now have marvellous facilities.

Ronnie Wolfenden

Warrington and the Navy

The town where I was born was Warrington and, well, we just lived for rugby. It was our main game in the streets or in the parks, touch rugby and so on. I've pretty much lived and breathed rugby all my life. Even then I think it meant more to us than what it means now, because there's a lot of hype about the game now. Then it was a beacon in the darkness of the depressed 1930s.

You talked about the game on Saturday until the following Wednesday when the teamsheet came out for the next match and then you talked about the forthcoming match. For the unemployed, rugby league was a beacon in very drab days. You had memories of the great Jack Fish, pre-First World War, a man who was quite a legend in the town and in the game. Yes, Warrington was very much focused on rugby league. I went to an all-age Catholic school and I don't think we could have picked 13, so we had very few team games. We did manage to raise a soccer side and I played soccer for the town. I found soccer very interesting, but rugby league was like a religion.

At 16, I hadn't played any really organised rugby, I was still a parks and back street player, but I went for trials with Warrington in 1936 and quite rightly I didn't get anywhere with it. I just wasn't good enough at that age and then, of course, the war came along. I went into the Navy, which meant that if you played rugby at all, it was rugby union. So I played rugby in the Navy, got picked for one or two Navy representative sides and I remember playing against a Kiwi side from the Middle East, led by Charlie Saxton, a great New Zealand captain. Bert Cook was stand-off half and Ike Procter played in the centre with the Navy team and Les Williams, who eventually signed for Hunslet, was playing for the Navy that day. I was enjoying rugby union, although rugby league was always the first choice if I could get a game.

Towards the end of the war, I was on a carrier, HMS Ocean, and we were off to Japan. But we were having some radio refitted in Gladstone dock, Liverpool and I drifted along to Liverpool Stanley, just to have a look at things. They were so short of players I found myself playing for them the next week. Quite an experience because they played two legs of the cup in those days; they were meeting Bradford Northern and I found myself opposite a chap named Ernest Ward who in the two legs scored I think it 45 individual points, which I think was then a world record.[5]
Joe Warham

A pretty tough life
I worked down t' pit all the time when I played. I was 14 [when I first went down the pit]. During the war, I used to work every Saturday morning and play rugby in the afternoon. Day shifts started a six o' clock in the morning 'till two. It was pretty tough really.
Frank Wagstaff

'Pinky' Klein and other Jewish players
Of course they couldn't play Saturdays, because that was against their religion, that's why Jewish people always gravitated towards Sunday sport, in those days there was no Sunday sport. Certainly Judeans

---

[5] In fact these were two league matches on consecutive weeks, won 41–4 and 67–0 by Bradford Northern in October 1945. Ernest Ward scored 20 points in the first game and 34 in the second.

have played on-and-off and there are names I can mention who were involved from a very early stage and went on to play for many other organisations. Although, [in Leeds] there are only two Jewish teams to my recollections, that's the Judeans and Leeds Jewish Institute, who used to play in the workshop [competitions] at Bus Vale, there are lots and lots and lots of Jewish players who played for non-Jewish teams. I can quote you lots of their names and the clubs they played for, some professional as well.

There's a guy who played before the war who's the father-in-law of a cousin of mine who rejoiced under the name of 'Pinky' Klein. He played for Bramley before the war. Everyone asks why they called him Pinky. The reason's quite simple, because no one could remember his English Christian name. But his Hebrew name was Pinkus, so everyone called him Pinky. There's another uncle of mine who played for Leeds several times in the late 1930s. His name was Monty White. He played several 'A' team games and looked like making a career for himself, when he broke his leg and couldn't play again.

He had a lot of problems because, you're talking about that generation, he was my mother's brother and their mother and father took a very dim view of it. In fact, my Grandma only spoke Yiddish, she couldn't speak English. So that gives you some idea of how recently they had come over from Lithuania.
Bernard Shooman

HMS Spiteful and the benefit of hard times
On my 18th birthday my mate Bill Robbie – he's dead and gone – a real gentlemen, he were 18 in May and I was 18 in June, this was 1942. We were having it a bit rough, he said to me "Come on, we're going to Leeds", he was a bit dominant like that. I said "Alright come on", no bus, we walked there. "New Station Street" he said. I said "Hold on, New Station Street, that's bloody Royal Naval isn't it, where they sign in for the Navy isn't it?" He said "Yes", I said "What are we doing here?" He said "We're signing up". "Oh" I said, "Thank you for telling us" but nevertheless I signed. So [when I got home], "Where have you been?" "Oh, I've joined the Navy", "Oh, have you?" That's all it was.

That's the difference with what would happen today. That's why people are different. Just did it, it was wartime you see and we were having it a bit rough. I was in for about four years, His Majesty's Submarine Spiteful. I went there and the next thing you know, it was the same old story of life now I realise I'm getting up to 84. They can kid you, we were 18 and the submarines was a volunteer service. It's understandable why, they couldn't get anybody, and just conned us.

The next thing I knew I had signed for the submarines. I had never seen t' sea before I joined the Navy, there I was signing. The average life expectancy at that time was 31½ days in the submarines in war there for eight to 10 years and I've been teetotal all my life. I've never drunk and you can imagine why. I saw people that drank in the club as a young lad. But I used to stay in the corner of the bar with my granddad and my uncle Tom and what they called the seniors.

The rugby men all sat in the right hand corner and I used to listen over the bar. So right from age 12 to whatever, 20 odd, I listened to all the great players. My granddad, my uncle Tom Schofield, there was Luke Nixon, a famous Featherstone player, Herbert Goodfellow, and his mates, Len Bratley from Wakefield, and Len Marshall used to come and I used to listen to them talking rugby.

So I had a great knowledge of rugby from all those fellows before me. I knew all the players. I knew all the teams and as a youngster. I used to take the rugby league results down for my dad from the wireless and I used to practice reading them. Barrow 6 Wakefield Trinity 14, Leeds 9 Hull Kingston Rovers 3. I used to read them and there was one that struck me. I didn't even know at the time what it would mean to me much later.

But my favourite one was listening to Bradford Northern 16 Wigan 7. That name, to me, Bradford Northern, was the most charismatic name there's ever been for any rugby team in the world and they've lost it. You can have whatever you like. Bradford Bulls means nothing. If they'd called it Bradford Northern Bulls fair enough. But Bradford Bulls means nothing.
Peter Fox

Ordinary working men
They worked in local jobs, I mean Alvin Ackerley, he was a drayman for Whitaker's brewery and when we were going to school Alvin would be there on the dray wagons and we'd see him. You'd see them in the streets. So there was a local affinity because they were working people. Alright they came from Wales – Les Pearce, Ronnie James, John Thorley – but they married and made their homes here and they became local people. Because they worked locally, you knew them; you saw them in the street, you looked up to them and you maybe aspired to be one of them.

They were part-time pros, but they played in big stadiums, played at Wembley; what a fantastic thing to play at Wembley, [and] Maine Road, Manchester when you could get 50,000 to 60,000 for a Championship Final, yet they were working alongside you, they worked in engineering shops. I never actually worked with any of the players, but I knew Charlie Renilson very well because he came in the pub. We watched *Match of the Day* on a Saturday night and his wife Thelma and my wife Val, they'd be in one corner having a natter and we'd be in the other corner watching *Match of the Day* cursing and swearing. But we were buddies.

Milan Kosanovic played for Bradford and Wakefield, but he had the chippy down our road. Then he bought a milk round and he was my in-laws' milkman. This guy had played in two Wembley cup finals and yet he's delivering milk. They were part of the community so for people like that there was an affinity, there but for the grace of god would go I. I was never good enough, it was as simple as that but at least you could rub shoulders with these people.
Geoff Wright

Half a day off on Tuesday
[After signing for Hull] they expected me to get over one day, Tuesday... In the winter we trained at Medley Street baths in Hull because we didn't train on the pitch there. But my day to do that was Tuesday. First of all I had to go into work and say "can I have half a day off on Tuesday?" I was a joiner by trade, serving my time then.

Luckily for me my boss was a former professional sportsman at soccer from West Hartlepool. So he said "I know the situation, boy, I don't mind, I can't pay you but you can have it off." So free of charge I used to finish work, wherever we were working, in time to get down to catch the 12.15 train at Tuesday dinner time from Leeds station to Hull. That got me in at 5 o'clock. I had to get from Paragon station at Hull to Medley Street baths in 15 minutes because training started at 5.30 and you couldn't be late when Roy Francis was concerned. Training lasted from 5.30 to 7.30 on the dot.

Then I had to get from Medley Street baths to Paragon station to catch the 7.55 train from Hull to Leeds. If I missed that I caught what was called the milk train which I think went as far up as Newcastle before it turned around [back to Leeds], it was some ridiculous way. I only did it once and it got me in at 1.15 in the morning. Catching my normal train at 7.55, I used to catch one of the last buses from City Square up Cardigan Road, when we lived in Harolds, and I used to be walking into my mother's house at 11.45 at night, from 12.15 at dinner time just to train.

Then Thursday they allowed me to train elsewhere, as long as I trained. But wherever I trained I had to get a chitty signed saying that I had been. For fitness training some clubs did allow it, just to [have a] run out. They didn't do any tactics because they didn't want you running back and telling the coach what they were going to do.
Maurice Bamford

Workmates
I worked in the engineers department at Lever Brothers and everybody was rugby mad. I mean, if I'd played well, then when I went into work on a Monday and my bench was packed, 'well done' and all this. But if I'd played bad, or they thought I'd played bad, there was no one there!

unbelievable really. They had a supermarket on the runway, bloody planes coming in at the side.

Went out there twice and rugby went into the background then. I got to 29, working away from home... up in Kendal in the Lake District. It was just a bit too much really. In fact Keighley said to me don't bother training. Bloody arse was on the floor on Saturday and you used to come back and probably go to Lancashire on the Saturday. Of course, my missus wasn't so pleased with two children and that.

Albert Eyre

Phoning in copy from Lawkholme Lane

When I came out of the army I started covering the rugby. I used to go down when I was working as a reporter, but I didn't always get the chance to cover the matches. I went back to the *Keighley News* because I'd worked there from school. I was covering... just general news reporting but I was always eager to get into sport. I went to grammar school and I just applied for the job.

I always sort of had covering sport at the back of my mind and I didn't know if it would ever materialise. I covered the amateur stage scene for a few years, used to be in a few Gilbert and Sullivan operas myself and a local church and amateur dramatic group. So that was another interest of mine. It wasn't until I moved to Bradford in 1968 that I really got into sport and covering sport full-time.

Originally when I started there [rugby league] was covered by a guy called Charlie Senior who was the chief reporter. He'd covered them pre-war, I think he'd been covering them [Keighley] when they went to Wembley in 1937. There wasn't anybody exclusively sport, it was all in amongst. Then a guy called Eric Lundy covered it for a long time, he died a few years ago. In fact as junior reporters we had to go down and phone copy from the press box at Keighley because they didn't have a direct phone line, but they used to have little phone booths under the stand. They were phoning for the *Yorkshire Sports Pink*, Saturday evening sports paper. Whoever was doing [the report] passed you the copy down.

So it was a way of getting into the match for nothing. But you missed quite a bit when you were phoning the copy. They'd be sending it every 15 to 20 minutes. That was one of the big differences. Nowadays it's straight onto a laptop. Then there was the mobile phone era or having fixed phones in press boxes, so it has all come along.

I remember going when mobile phones first came into use – you were carrying a bag round with the battery charger. I'd finished before they started doing that with the laptops, but it's certainly different these days. When I started doing the coverage at Keighley, I tried to alter it a bit because it was a weekly paper. All they used to do was give a match report and this was coming out a week later.

41

So it was a bit silly really, straight match report and the teams. I tried to still feature the match report, but to look ahead a bit and preview. I started travelling with the team a bit at Keighley, Harry Street was coaching. I'd chat with him, ring him up. Later he came to Bradford of course, met up with him there.

Bradford played at Castleford; they were having a bad spell at the time. It would be about November and they got beat [heavily]. I wrote a fairly critical piece, can't remember what I said, but I remember Harry ringing me up and saying "Are you trying to get rid of me?" I think he did finish fairly soon after that, this was at Bradford about 1970.[7]

Brian Smith

G.F. Potts

There was a very famous sports editor at the *Pontefract and Castleford Express* called George Potts – G.F. Potts. Now, Potts was a legend because not only was he a huge imposing man in a great coat who drove a Jaguar. I mean for somebody in Pontefract and Featherstone that in itself was another thing.

I used to go with him and not only did he do reports for the *Pontefract and Castleford Express* and was the sports editor, but he did the first of those one minute rugby league reviews from Woodhouse Lane, BBC North, that went out on the *Look North* programme. That is where I got my first taste of broadcasting. I used to go down with him and we used to go into this room and he did it live, we used to go straight after the Featherstone match.

He was such an imposing man. Post Office Road in Featherstone, there's a very wide car park before you go into the gate itself and he was a bit like Messiah was George Potts. As the Jaguar used to go into the car park, there was someone always there saluting as the gates opened. I never forget there was one game, an important game, and they had a lot more security. He pulled in his Jaguar and the gates didn't open and the man had the temerity to say to him "Who are you?" I don't think that man had a job after that day.

It's a very small and compact ground and the arrangements for the press were very interesting. It was a five-person press box and anybody who's been to Featherstone and been up to the top of the stands on a winter's day will know just how bleak it is up there. Now some of the press days used to get a lot of interest from people. For instance some former sporting stars used to report rugby league for some of the papers and this particular day there was Bill Bowes, the former Yorkshire and England bowler who was writing for the *Evening News* and Fred Trueman was writing for the *Post.*

---

[7] Bradford lost 58–12 at Castleford on 13 December 1972

There were only five places and there was George Potts and myself, and George allocated the places. I sat next to Bill Bowes and Freddie Trueman had to sit outside, I'll never forget, which he didn't like very much because it was a bleak day on this cup game with 5,000 in the ground. It was that kind of local hierarchy as well and always organised by with the local press baron in those situations. In other words no one violated your press box and he said who went in.

There am I sitting next to Bill Bowes, talking about cricket and Australia and eating humbugs. It was a memorable occasion. Bowes, of course, had long retired, but he became quite a well-known journalist. Trueman, I think, had just finished that short one-day spell with Derbyshire, so it was late 1960s and he was just starting his writing career and did some rugby league.

Chris Hawksworth

1970 to 1995

The Halifax Pop and Blues Festival

Well I'd been quite close to the club [Halifax], but not in a working capacity, I'd recommended one or two players to them who I knew about. It was quite exciting really. I remember the first night when I went to my first board meeting, the then chairman, a man named Horsefall, who was a local architect in Halifax, sat me down and told me the whys and wherefores, what I should do and what I shouldn't do. After about 12 months you become a seasoned director, you become more knowledgeable.

I had one very big experience at Halifax while I was on the board. We were very hard up, that was before we won the Regal Trophy and we were thinking about schemes to raise money. The team wasn't all that good and the gates were falling. So I came home from a board meeting one night... at the time my children were probably around 13 or 14.

I said "What do you think about having a pop concert at Thrum Hall?" There had been a big one and we could do a far better job because we had a stadium, it's enclosed you see. They thought it was a wonderful idea and of course they all knew the best pop acts. I didn't know a thing about them and it took off from there. I appointed an agent who lived in Doncaster and took it to the board and they were "Oh what do you want a pop concert for?" "Well to make money, it's the in thing." I finally persuaded them that we should have it and we fixed a date, 8 April.

We got this agent and got some marvellous bands. We got Fleetwood Mac, Marmalade, Tremeloes, Chicken Shack, Salt and Pepper and the greatest show on earth, the compere Lee Travis and the guy in Leeds, Jimmy Saville. It cost a heck of a lot of money so it had to be a success. We thought we'd get 30,000 to 40,000 in. The stadium itself had had, for a football match, about 32,000 and of course you could use part of the field so we thought "The sky's the limit", we might get 40,000 to 50,000 given the weather was fine.

Blow me, it was the worst possible weather it could have been. It snowed and blew for a full week right up till the Saturday morning. In fact at one stage it looked as though we'd have to cancel it completely because the ground was a quagmire. We'd got our agents all over, we'd sent tickets down as far south as Birmingham, Leicester, out to Newcastle, Liverpool the east coast, Hull, we got no end of agents. On the day it was so bad, we had an attendance just short of 3,000 so we lost a lot of money on it.
Ronnie Wolfenden

Man management
My business was knowing players. I was a man manager at work that was my job. I was a training and safety officer at IMI, Imperial Metal Industries, in Leeds and I was the apprentice training manager. I trained 420 engineering apprentices in my career and I was the shop steward for Group 2 when I was a draughtsman. I was head of the union when I was at the Copper Works. I got [the union] going a BJD first and I got all the engineers into it at the Copper Works.

When I left school I went to BJD as an apprentice engineer. You served time in different shops. I served it in the machine shop. From the machine shop I applied for a draughtsman's job at 19 and the boss of the drawing office was a fellow called Archie Rawning, who happened to be in the church choir at Sharlston that I was in. So I'm not saying that I was favoured, but I don't think it did me any harm!

I got appointed into the drawing office at BJD, served my time out and got a regular job in the drawing office of the mining division, detailed draughtsman on mining machinery. Stayed there a few years and then got this job at IMI as a draftsman. When I became the training and safety officer I was doing training programmes for senior engineers, supervisors and mangers. So I was dealing with people all my life and I went on several courses, man management courses to Portsmouth, I went for six weeks.

I believe in one thing. You be honest with me and I'll be honest with you. I'll trust you and tha's two chances. Tha can let me down once, but if tha lets me down a second time tha's finished. I had that with every player and I didn't have many problems at all. I had 400 and odd apprentices and I only had to sack one. I didn't sack him, but my boss sacked him. With the Copper Works apprentices [aged] between 15 and 20 [as they] became engineers, they were all under my control even though they were out in the works. I had to look after their homework and their school work, and guide them everywhere. So I got great rapport with the lads and I always had that with the players.

I didn't coach for money, I coached for the involvement and liking the players and I got on well with all my players' wives and girlfriends. If they had a problem with their husbands they came to me and I sorted it out. So I was well thought of by all the girls as well. I've never let a player down in my life... If I had to get rid of one I got him a job. I didn't sack him and say "I'm sorry", I found a place for him wherever I went, at any club I was with.

Peter Fox

From Cape Town to Hemsworth

I moved to Hemsworth in 1972 and fitted in straight away. Not forgetting, people ask "Did you have problems with racism?" I had problems in South Africa. In England, well, people may have called me things, but nobody stopped you from getting what you wanted.

There was no restriction of what you could and couldn't do. You lived in a country where you were free as long as you didn't commit crimes. But if you don't make yourself part of the community, if you don't integrate, if you don't offer, if you don't participate, if you don't get involved in the culture, if you don't get involved with people, well you're going to be isolated.

You need to show the community you're part of it, and part of a community is about participation and understanding. My father-in-law was a gentleman who never looked at race. He looked at people about ability. I became virtually his son.

He loved rugby league, he loved coming to the games. My wife had four sisters and I don't know if you've seen the *Royle Family*. Every Sunday it was like that in their house and it was fantastic. For me it was an excellent experience because it was about family support. Lucky for me I came into a family where I was part of it and it was nothing about colour.

I used to go to the shop where we lived on Barnsley Road and I would come home two hours later. My wife would say "David, where have you been?" I would say "I've just been to the shop for a paper". She would say "But you left at seven 'o' clock. Do you know what time it is? It's nine 'o' clock." I said "How can I walk past anybody who wants to engage with me and all they want to talk about is rugby." I can't say "I can't talk to you", it's a village and people talk to each other. We had a fruit and vegetable shop in Hemsworth and the guy used to say "Dave, what fruit do you eat?" and I said "Well I eat mangos" and he used to bring this fruit in.

David Barends

A matter of principle

By the time I resigned [as a Halifax director], if I hadn't resigned I would have been chairman the following year. I didn't want to resign at all, but we felt on a point of principle we had to. It was a terrible time. We had such a good side; we'd just won the Players No.6 Trophy. When we beat Leeds at Headingley in the semi-final, this was a tremendous day.

Leeds had not lost at Headingley for two years and we beat them fairly easily that day and my two young daughters were in the crowd, not with me, we were in the stand, directors' seats, but I remember them running across Headingley field, they were absolutely delighted when the final whistle went. It was unfortunate. I think there were 10 directors at the time and it was the younger end, obviously I was a lot younger then, that resigned. We said that the older ones and some of them at the time were in their 70s, will sell players to survive now because they haven't the ability to get around and scout and do the job they were supposed to do.

They did in fact, they sold players one by one and within two years Halifax finished at the bottom of the league and they hadn't won a solitary game in 1974–75 season. They hadn't won a solitary game right up to the middle of March. Of course then the season started in September. They had played something like played 24 games lost 24 and that was from a really cracking side, because they had just sold players to survive. It was an awful job recovering the club.
Ronnie Wolfenden

King of the factory
I didn't socialise too much because, some of the lads, there were drinkers and then there were drinkers, and we had a few Welshmen in the team who could drink a bit. In those days I'd just got married and I couldn't afford to be stopping out till all hours. It wasn't just from the money aspect it was that you didn't want to do it, you had to get up for work. There was a hell of a lot of that culture, a hell of a lot. But I'm not knocking it. I don't know what it is like now but there were some bloody drinkers about in them days.

I worked alongside the supporters and when you had a good game it was nice, but when you had a poor game, these guys used to tell you about it. It was good in one way because you were all fighting the same cause. They were supporters and they didn't want you to have bad games and they didn't want to be kicking your arse on a Monday morning after you'd played on a Sunday, like a don't know what.
They'd much prefer to come into work on a Monday morning and pat you on the back rather than kick you up the backside. You enjoyed it. It made your working week a lot more pleasant when you'd had a good game on the Sunday because for the remainder of the week you were the king in the factory.

It was good, I suppose it's like when I used to read about the old-time footballers who used to travel on the same bus. Stanley Matthews used to go and travel with the supporters on a match day and they'd

46

Bak Diabira (on right) playing against the Australians for Blackpool in 1978.
(Courtesy *Rugby League Journal*)

be cheering him from the stand and they'd been on the same bus going to the match with him. People say to me "I bet you begrudge what they're getting paid now don't you" and I say "no" because I know how hard it is. I don't care how much them lads are getting paid, they deserve every penny of it and good luck to them. I just hope the majority of them look after it right. It's a short career and I was never a full-time professional, but I didn't do too badly. I never got international recognition because I was unable to[8], maybe even if I had been able to I wouldn't have been good enough but at the end of the day I didn't too badly.
Bak Diabira

Crossing the tracks
I worked at the pit. I was a fitter underground. Jimmy Thompson worked with me as well and what we used to do was, [at] Featherstone, the pit was on one side of the lane and there was a bridge across and Post Office Road was on the other side of the road. When we were on afternoons we used to, in us overalls, nip across the railway line, on to the training pitch, do us training and put us overalls back on and nip back over the railway line and go back to the pit. [Our workmates] knew, yeah. They were all right with it.

[During the 1985 miners strike] you had no money. My mum used to get ration bags with tins and stuff for you to eat because you'd got

[8] Diabira was born in Bordeaux, and therefore was not qualified to play for Great Britain.

no money. What you did was, because you didn't buy houses in them days, you were renting council houses. They'd hold your rent back so you hadn't to pay your rent and then when you went back to work they let you start paying it then. People still went and watched, because in them days there was no other entertainment, it was either rugby or the club. That was it. It was about 12 months, a long time. I was playing rugby as well, so I wasn't so bad.
Keith Bridges

Travelling on the team bus
A pal of mine had been doing the job, [at the *Telegraph and Argus*] a guy called Barry Wood who was offered a job at the *Daily Sketch*. I think [the *Telegraph and Argus*] must have asked him if there was anyone he could recommend. I was approached and I jumped at it really. It was another two pound a week or something like that.

I didn't have a car at the time, so I used to travel on the team bus occasionally, as was the trend with the local reporter, which was handy in some ways. At that time, being the age I was, you were on the same level as some of the players in some respects and you got quite friendly with a lot of them. But I never felt it sort of restricted me and I only ever really had two or three players over the years that really got nasty about something. When you used to go on the team bus it was a bit strange, because if you were coming back from Lancashire they'd usually stop somewhere like Hebden Bridge, or wherever, for a pint and they would pick up the *Yorkshire Sports*, you see. If they were coming back from York or the East Coast they could pick up the *Evening Post* green edition and it was a bit daunting sometimes [because] I used to do a comment piece.

You knew they were sitting reading what you'd written and it was a strange feeling. But by and large I think they accepted you'd to do your job and you weren't being malicious. I felt you had to give an opinion. I think this is one thing I sort of regret these days. I think, with all due respect and there are one or two exceptions, it's sort of programmed a bit too much now, the journalism, and it's very rare for people to come out and say something. I don't mean you've to be negative, but I think you've got to reflect a bit of the fans' side of it and if they're not playing well, say so. There had to be trust really. I didn't want to tell tales out of school. I would never have done that. But the whole concept's changed really. These lads were working hard during the week and playing rugby. I don't think they're necessarily better players these days. There are some good players, I'm not saying there aren't. But the fitness is tremendous isn't it? It's a completely different game, even from the 1970s and the 1980s. It's changed completely.
Brian Smith

Family support

My dad was quite a sporty individual. He was, in the old days, an armchair observer of *Grandstand* [on television], he wouldn't move. His sport was boxing. He used to box in the Pakistani Air force before he came to this country. I'm certain that's where we get our physical side, all my brothers. Even my sisters, he encouraged them to take part in rounders and netball and they did it quite well.

I remember he bought us junior boxing gloves. Me and our Tony and our young'un, we used to box in the room and sometimes me and our young'un used to fight with Tony because he was a bit bigger than us. He was two years older than us and then me and our young'un used to fight with each other. I remember coming home from school sometimes bumps and bit of blood.

My mam would mother cuddle us, but my dad, his question was: "Did you give it as good as you get?" I know my other friends, not just Asian origin, but the diverse groups they had [at our school], their parents would discourage them from taking part in rugby because it was physical. It was tough, it was a sport that they weren't too much into and kept away from. The reason why we excelled can only be the fact that my father was very sporty. He was keen to try any sports and that's where we got our encouragement from.

Interesting thing, though, my mam's quite a big sport fan too, but she never watched my dad box and she'd never seen us play apart from in the back yard. But that was probably a cultural thing. My sisters, nieces and kids, they'd regularly come to watch when possible. But then my parents were first generation. My dad was one of a few Asian parents coming to watch, there were others, but very few and it's sad.

When my father passed away my eldest brother was living in Denmark. So Tony had to be the breadwinner for the family and that was great for me because it allowed me to concentrate more on my rugby. So he sort of sacrificed his career for me which I owe him a lot for to this day. We're brothers of course and very close. Good mates and he is still very supportive. Had my father been alive things might have been different, we might have had that support. There's always a reason why and it's a shame that, after he was no more, we didn't have that support and encouragement, but no regrets. Things happen for a reason and I suppose that's one of the reasons why we were so determined to succeed.

That determination, self-belief and school of thought to do well and do your best was inspired by my father. I would say that because way back in the early days he was a hard but fair man, well disciplined. He gave us a lot of rope in regards to trying new things, but he was disciplined and I think that helped us a great deal. My dad was quite religious and that was really important to us and still is now.

I'm no saint, but it plays a big part in the focus and mental strength of self-belief and determination. But it's also important that when you are doing something to be aware about others and have that genuine care. Yes, you want to succeed but not at all costs. You've got to treat people as you expect to be treated and that's a really important aspect, particularly when you're playing. But also when you're trying to set an example to other young people, you've got to walk the walk and talk the talk, so to speak. You've got to set an example. When you're in the spotlight and when you're having a role where particularly children and young people look up to you, you've got to lead by example.

Ikram Butt

For the love of the game

The directors left the club in dispute with the chairman, a bit of an extrovert and controversial type of figure, he actually just wanted the pavilion for a nightclub, nothing else, he wasn't interested in rugby. He tried to get money off all the rest of the directors to pay for new kitchen equipment, instead of putting it into rugby so they all said "Goodbye, we're rugby people". It had folded up. John Bailey found out that he was losing money on rugby and that in his lease he only had to play rugby league as a professional or amateur to keep his pavilion. He said he was going to go amateur. Me and my dad said "You can't do that, [Huddersfield] is one of the most famous clubs in the league plus it's the birthplace of rugby league. To have no professional rugby in this town would be a shame."

He took it on board and thought "Well yes, you're right, I'll continue but I can't continue for long. You've put a lot of hard work in with your family over the years and it would be unfair of me, [so] you carry on until someone takes over," which we did.

We put an advert in the papers, we wrote to local businessmen including Lord Hanson, people like that: not interested. Crowds started to fall down to 200 to 300, people couldn't understand why we weren't buying players. I had no money as I was only a maintenance engineer at Huddersfield Polytechnic.

It carried on and [we reached] the last ditch. I was talking in Runcorn in the boardroom to a chap who I didn't know. He was the editor of the *Rugby Leaguer* and he put an advert in for nothing: "Could somebody take over this once proud and famous club." Mick Murphy, who played for St Helens, and had a string of hotels in Aberdeen for the oil rig people, saw the advert, answered it, we met him on a Thursday night in Fartown and thank goodness he took over because three days after that the club would have folded.

That was the deadline and there wouldn't have been a Huddersfield Rugby League Club ever again. If they had moved out, amateurs would have moved in, if anybody wanted to set up a professional club,

3.   Playing

Before 1945

The *Sports Echo* boots

There was a famous paper, the *Sports Echo*, and they used to award a pair of boots to who they thought was the most promising schoolboy in the area and I managed to win a pair. [This was] 1935, I'd be about 12 years old, [and playing] for Hunslet National School. Every school in the area played rugby league. There was only one school, Hunslet Moor, which didn't play rugby, they played soccer and were the only soccer team in the area. Within a stone's throw of one another there was Hunslet National, Low Road, Hunslet Carr, Dewsbury Road, South Accommodation Road and everybody used to play one another. Unfortunately, most of the matches used to be played up at Middleton Clearing, which was in the middle of a great big wood, Middleton Woods. We used to have to get up there by going on the tram. The tram used to stop halfway up through the wood and you had to get off and walk up the path onto the top to the clearing. There were wooden huts where you could get changed and that was about all. If it was muddy or wet you had to wait until you got home to get washed and changed and that's how we were brought up to play rugby.

Because it was the weekend, when the match finished the teacher wanted somebody to take the ball and bring it back on Monday morning. Invariably, I used to get the ball and in the evening we'd be out with our mates with the ball playing touch-and-pass. Someone would shout "'Ey up, there's a bus coming", because we were on one of the main bus routes. Of course, we'd just stand back, let the bus come by and carry on with what we were doing. That's how we were brought up.
Frank Watson

Workmates for the backs

My job was to get the ball from the scrum. It's a changed game now. But if I got half possession, clubs were happy; it didn't matter about me scoring tries. Well you couldn't score tries because we used to hold each other in – the front-row men. I was a field-side prop. I used to follow the ball in and kick it back, I was good at it. I used to play in the second-row and then when I put weight on I played in the front-row. I started at 13 stone and went to 18 stone. I don't know why, but I did. I was just right for the front-row, just right weight. I used to score a few tries when I was in the second-row. In fact the first match I played for Huddersfield I scored three tries in the second-row.

Of course I was lucky, when I started in the front-row I played with some old hookers that learned me all the tricks and there were some tricks and all [such as] getting the scrum-halves to put ball in right, give it a spin. Spin it your way. That was one trick. I got away with it with most refs, you know, hooking the ball back. It was supposed to be the hooker's job, you see. I think playing football helped my rugby. I was always fit. I ... didn't smoke, didn't drink much either. I was a good tackler because I learnt at school, we were always wrestling and boxing at school, so tackling came as a gift really. In the forwards we had to get the ball for the backs, they said they didn't want to bring wing men from Australia and not give 'em the ball because you can't play without the ball. We were workmates for the backs.

Frank Wagstaff

Playing rugby league football

We'd 13 players, there was no tactics. You went out to play. You weren't told to watch him or watch him, none of that at all, you just went to play rugby. This is what annoys me, all these so-called managers telling them [today's players] how to play. Well you play according to what's going on. You're playing rugby league football. Bill Hannah was the trainer. There was no tactics talked or anything like that. You went training Tuesday and Thursday and played Saturday. [We used to] run around the cricket pitch and there was very little ball stuff. He worked on the theory, did Billy Hannah, that you played with the ball on the field.

Sid Rookes

Wanting to play for Hunslet

At 14 we left school and then anybody interested in rugby went on to Parkside to Hunslet. They used to run a 14s to 16s junior team and you joined them. Two local fellows used to coach us. One of them was Fred Dobson, brother of the famous referee from Featherstone, Frank Dobson. Then you carried on to the 16s to 18s, by which time a lot of lads used to lose interest as they found work and things like that. But I was so keen I wanted to carry on with the idea of wanting to play with Hunslet at Parkside.

I did about two seasons in the 16s to 18s team and then just before the war, 1939, I was invited up into the committee rooms, which were in the old Parkside pavilion. I think it was Mr Meeks who was the chairman then, it could have been Mr Wilson, and I had to bring an adult with me. My father, he wasn't at home at that time, so I took a chap with me who had no idea of rugby, but he was an adult. I'm at this end of the table looking down. It looked a mile long, the chairman at the [other] end and directors at each side saying "We would like you to sign on for the club. We'll give you £100, but we'll give you £10 now and the rest when [wartime] hostilities cease." So fair enough, money didn't particularly matter, [it was] the fact that you were signing for Hunslet, you know. So there it was I signed.

Frank Watson

Events that changed my world

I was 17 when I signed for Morecombe [at football]. I must have been reasonably good. I was in defence, left full-back. I got good write ups for a young player and I thought that was going to be my career really. There were scouts, [who] used to follow me about and there was one man from Bury. They [Bury] had an idea that if they bought young players and sold them on, like. Colin Bell started with Bury. That's the idea of it and with me being 18, they were looking for youngsters. He used to come through to Barrow to our house and talk and he got me a match against Liverpool. I must have had a good game because Liverpool came in then.

On 2 September [1939] I played against Blackpool for Liverpool and the evening paper said "Knowelden made an auspicious debut". Now what does auspicious mean? My dad and I didn't know what auspicious meant! We had to get the dictionary out when we got home and it said very promising. That was on the Saturday and on 3 September war broke out and my world had finished. But I was talking to a lad in Blackpool, Gerry Wolstenholme, the other day and he said "Just look, you might never have got to Wembley and you wouldn't have got to Australia if you'd been a footballer. It changed your world."

I started in the 1943–44 season, so it was four years [later], I was 23, when I started rugby. I think it was good time to start. It's like my brother always said "You missed going through the rough and the tough, you're fit, you've never had an injury in your life, you're in your prime." In a way, when I started I was playing against people who were just on the verge of finishing. Fred Harris of Leeds, Stanley Brogden, they were on their way out and they were very good. I remember Fred Harris coming and shaking my hand when I played against him, "Well done son," he said and he would be about perhaps 33 or 34, you see. So it was a good time to come in and get settled into a position.

Bryn Knowelden

Get the ball up

At Hunslet, Les White played hooker and before we came out he'd come and get hold of me and say "Now then Frank, when you get up to the pack, get the ball up, throw the ball up". Of course, in those days the hooker would have what you called the 'loose arm' and if you didn't get it up he'd give you a bit of a rollicking. Sometimes you'd to get up and block the referee's view into the pack, get up as close as you could. But many a time the whistle would go and he gave a free kick.

Frank Watson

Not turning anybody down

The war came and Castleford closed down. I went to Huddersfield as a guest player. I wanted to go to get some experience, which I did get. I got better paid as well during the war. I used to get good expenses. Huddersfield paid £8 for a win and £6 for a loss. I was delighted to go to Huddersfield, it was a club I liked, it was a good team [with] a lot of guest players, internationals. We used to get in nearly every cup final with Dewsbury; they had a better team than us. Clubs packed up during the war, you see, I can't just remember 'em all now. But Dewsbury were a good side. Huddersfield approached Castleford for me and if Huddersfield hadn't a match I could play with another team. I think I [went] to Hull three times in three weeks. I used to get a telegram on a Friday if Huddersfield hadn't a game, "Would I go?" like. I didn't turn anybody down. I played with Batley, Keighley, quite a few times, when I was free. I got to know a lot of players. Nobody seemed to want to play at Hull!

Frank Wagstaff

First impressions

The most impressive thing that I found, and something that stood me in good stead, was the play-the-ball. In rugby union the mauls and scrimmages are a great part of the game. In rugby league, with having six forwards and a play-the-ball when you were tackled, everybody had to move back so many yards, five yards in those days – it gave a lot more fresh air you might say – you were not one on top of each other. The mauls in rugby union were really stoppages in play, negative, as compared with standing back in rugby league. You were one-to-one. You were tackled by your opposite number. You had to play-the-ball as quickly as you could and go forward. That was much better than going into rucks and mauls.

[The players] were most friendly, [there was] outstanding friendliness, help and advice from veterans of the game; where to stand in certain positions and as regards scrimmaging, how to get down and make the most of your weight in the scrum. In the dressing room and off the field they were very keen to see you settled in, you'd come from a long way away – most wonderful comrades. The strangeness of the game, particularly in the pack after the rucks and mauls, was completely new. But I found a lot of space around the middle of the field with only six forwards as against eight. I can remember getting a pass under my own goal posts and I kicked the ball and it went 40 or 50 yards into touch. The crowd clapped and clapped and gave the impression this chap knows what rugby league football is all about and I never kicked a ball since! We lost [my first game]. But in the newspapers, the critics were saying 'this laddie looks good, he's well built and he looks like he'll become a useful player.'

Trevor Foster

58

give me a chance to get to know any of the other lads and things so I signed. There was nothing really I could do.

This was the end of 1950 so it was quite a lot of money and the standard of pay was £8 for a win, £5 for a loss. He said "Sign" and £250 looked a lot of money, so I signed. When I got into the dressing room the players said "What have you done Len?" I said "Well I've signed", "How much did you get?" "£250," "You're crazy, you could have got that £1,000 they offered you in the past. The reason he met you at the gates, he didn't want you to see us to put you straight!"
Len Haley

You reap what you sow
Pete Hanson [was] a very tough lad, born in Hunslet. He's dead now, but [was] a hard man, played in the centre and then moved into the forwards, we played at Dewsbury together. We were travelling to play Hull and they had a fearsome pack at the time. Pete was playing loose-forward and I was playing blindside prop then. Pete came and sat beside me on the bus. He said "Are you all right, young 'un?" I said "You all right Peter?" "Yeah," he

said "Are you looking forward to it today?" I said "I am." He said "There might be one or two looking after you, you know". I said "Aye, I think so." He said "Jim Drake will be after you, because you'll be playing opposite Jim," he said. "Be careful of him close in, he sticks nut on you." I said "Yeah, OK Peter, thanks very much." He stopped talking and sat back in the chair and said "Do you know what I was taught at an early age Maurice? No matter how big the man, if he hits you, it doesn't hurt you for the rest of your life. That hurt goes away in few minutes. So there's nothing to be afraid of." That was his philosophy and I thought it was good one to preach to a kid.

Even today, rugby league football's a brutal game. It's harder than rugby union because there's more one-on-ones. Rugby union's dangerous I think. I've known a lot of lads in rugby league who would have killed in rugby union with the rucking and mauling, where until recently you were allowed to ruck an opposing player. Brutal men. But when the whistle goes that's the end. "I've just knocked seven bells out of you, but come on get this pint this down you, cheers old lad." You'd be right as rain until next time you saw me when you played at our place. I'll level you, first tackle because that was the nature of the game. It was a brutal game. Nobody moaned, you didn't say "he's hit me," you did your share.

What you reap you sow and if you didn't have that mongrel streak in you, you were playing the wrong game. But you didn't carry that mongrel streak throughout your life. You carried it for 80 minutes on a weekend and then you were Mr Normal, you were Jekyll and Hyde and most players were. God love him, Trevor Foster spoke of how every time he played against Arthur Clues, Arthur gave him a good hiding. Yet he was always the first to him at the bar and he invited Trevor and his wife to Sunday dinner at his house. They were marvellous friends. But next time he played against him, he gave him a good hiding did Arthur, because he wanted winning money. It was all based on money, all based on how much you got. If you could see off a top player, like Willie Horne at Barrow, if you could get to him early on, give him a clout and remove him. There were no subs then and not only were they playing 12 men, but they'd lost their king pin. Tactics of games were built around things like that.
Maurice Bamford

Photo of Maurice Bamford by David Williams (rlphotos.com)

My move
I was more of a runner than a defender. With the ball in my hands I was a strong runner. When I was 17 we were playing up at Roundhay, with the juniors and we were playing the ball, Bernard Prior was acting half-back. I just looked for a gap and I thought "Right". I didn't tell anybody I was doing anything, just came from the back, not in the line, but from deep. As soon as they played the ball I set off. Bernard was looking at the first receiver, he wasn't looking at me and I wanted to intercept that ball as Bernard passed it. Do you know nobody used to see you because where he's looking they look. They know who's getting the ball, just the same as we do. So they're all going for him. But you come in short and hard, for some reason they just don't notice you're coming. You're 20 yards back when you set off, they've discarded you. But I've never told anybody that.

I thought that if I tell anybody else and they know how to do it, they'll all be trying it. It was my move. I scored a lot of tries off that. Our own players used to say "Where have you come from?" The only thing was, if you didn't time it right, you could either be short or too far up and in that case you'd got to let the ball go and get out of the way. But it was very rare I didn't get to t' ball. I suppose it's just a knack of knowing where your players move. Because without looking involved in fights and that sort of business. But I had to stand up for myself.

Then, of course, when one or two other people came out and we had an Other Nationalities match against a Sydney team we played at the cricket ground. I think it was before a test match. Lewis [Jones] was there and Dick Huddart. We'd no coach and somebody said "How are we going to play this match?" Dick Huddart said "I don't care. I just want to square a few accounts." We got beat I think, but we were very satisfied when we came off, because there was a bunch of us Poms that could all stand up for each other, rather than just being on your own and everybody saying [it was] "hit the Pom week".

The lifestyle [the] Australians are now trying to sell sun and barbecues. There's more to it than that, you've got to go to work. You don't go to the beach every day. It was not a lot different from here. You worked and you went out and socialised. You spent a bit more time outside probably.
Derek Hallas

Roy's vision
It was great playing the sort of style that Roy [Francis] wanted us to play, which was play football in any part of the field. One of the things he pointed out to me was [when] he drew a rugby field and said "What's that?" I said "It's a rugby field." Then he said "Which part of that rugby field does it say you have to play certain type of game?" I said "Well it doesn't." He said "Exactly, it's a rugby field, you can play rugby in any part of that field." I've scored tries from when I've been stood on my own line and we've opened the ball out, because that's what he bred in us. It's a rugby field. We don't play this kind of rugby in that 25, you don't play that type in that bit or the other type in the other bit. You play rugby right the way through the field. If you're stood on your own line and there are gaps, you attack the gaps. You don't just play a style of rugby because you're on your own line and that was instilled into us from the very first with Roy and it worked.

I just played a little bit under the unlimited [tackles rule] and then it was four tackles, but he never worked a theory out because it was four tackles. He wasn't about kicking or anything like that. He said if we do kick it, we can kick it just as equally on the first tackle as on the fourth, it's about what advantage we're going to get out of kicking the ball. The forwards used to take the mickey out of me for kicking on the first tackle and I used to say "How many wages have we won because I kicked on the first tackle?" But it was about what Roy had instilled, plus your own vision.
John Atkinson

Signing for Leeds

I went to Leeds when I was 23, the back end of 1967 in June I signed, and in 68 we were at Wembley. I was Very lucky, really, but in a good team. I wanted to get away from Keighley because I was a bit stagnated and I was playing quite good rugby at the time. Wakefield were interested, I think, and Bradford Northern and Leeds came on the scene. Of course my brother was there then, he'd already gone from Hunslet.

I signed with Leeds and saw Roy Francis who told me what he wanted, what he expected and what his hopes were and they all came true. That's why I couldn't wait to go and I didn't want to go to anywhere else; not because my brother Kenny was there. He was there and that was it, it wasn't because my brother was there.

...he explained to me that they were hoping to get Billy Ramsey from Hunslet which he did do eventually after I'd signed. But Billy was the last cog in the machine that played all as one as he put it to me. That was the squad that had the best four years Leeds have had I think. They've had good times since then, but it was a good time to be there.

A lot of it goes over your head because everything is that fast. When we went to any big games there was a ticket for the wife and everything was organised, you do it yourself normally. Your families were looked after, even those with children. It's still a great club.

Billy Ramsey came from Hunslet and that was the last signing of that team and everybody gelled together. There was a lot of Hunslet lads in it, Billy Ramsey, my brother, myself, Mick Shoebottom, Sid Hynes, Barry Seabourne and they were all from Hunslet. It's strange really how it all turned out. I'm not saying that's the reason why it was a good team, but the nucleus of that team was from Hunslet.

As I say I was 23, another two years at Keighley and I would have been due for a benefit. It was ridiculous really ... benefits in those days – they got £350 at Keighley. I didn't play for money, I never did, but it was a big thing to go to a better club. When you read in the papers that clubs are interested in you, that's when it starts to upset players and obviously you were in touch with Leeds players; playing against them. We used to travel on the train to Keighley, a crowd of us – Crookson and Alfie Barren. We used to go to the West Riding pub at the end of Wellington Street in Leeds and all the Leeds lads were there. After matches everybody used to trail down there.

Anybody refusing to go to Leeds needed their heads testing. They talk about back handers in the game, not saying that they didn't go on, because I know they did. Anybody who refused to go to Leeds because they didn't get a back hander must have been absolutely off their rocker. I don't know many who did, but if they did they wanted their heads testing because they didn't know what they were missing.

scored on the cricket pitch. He went under the posts. They were playing Salford, by the way, and Salford had a good side. In them days there were some good teams, 10 at least, five from either county.
Stanley Pickles

At the centre of life in Warrington
[In the 1930s] Wilderspool was very different. First of all you had to cross a railway line over Bridgefoot. There was nearly always a train coming and, because the goods wagons were shunting back and forth, the railway line could be closed for quite some time. So the harsh decision when you got there, and the gates were closed, was should I go over the pedestrian bridge, because sod's law declared that when you were halfway up there, the gates would open down below. Then you had to walk across a field at the back of St James's Church. I don't know what it is now, but then it was just spare ground and on this spare ground there would be, well it was a little like a medieval fair I suppose. There were the vendors selling cough tablets, Uncle Joe's' mint balls or whatever they were, and there were escapologists performing.

I remember a little knot of people around someone who was telling them about the Marie Stopes method or something or other and promising you diagrams of the female genitalia and we were ushered away from all this. We used to go an hour before kick-off. We got in for tuppence and the boys' pen was behind the sticks at the railway end. You had to get into it through the crowd and you just couldn't get through the crowd if you were late. So they used to pick you, pass you over the heads of the crowd and drop you into the boys' pen. But as I say, it was the highlight of the week and not just the game – we went to training sessions. Without Wilderspool there wasn't life in Warrington.
Joe Warham

Gambling on a draw
[When] I started watching them [Halifax] on a regular basis, I think we used to pay two old pennies to go into the ground at Thrum Hall. They had some pretty good sides leading up to the Second World War, particularly in 1936, '37, '38 and '39, just before the outbreak of war.

In fact they won the last rugby league Cup Final at Wembley before the outbreak of war when they beat Salford quite easily, I think that was something like 20–3. Salford were virtually an all international side, they had 12 internationals and one county player. They were overwhelming favourites to beat Halifax and Halifax walloped them. At the time or just before, it would about 1937 I think, Halifax signed [some] Maori players from a club called Streatham & Mitcham in London. There were two clubs at the time in London, one called

Streatham & Mitcham and the other Acton & Willesden. They were good sides, but as always it never really took off in London. Two good sides, but playing in front of very small crowds.

They both linked up one season, I think it would be about 1936, and Halifax stepped in and signed [some] of their best players. They included a man named Charlie Smith, a huge centre threequarter, about six foot three and 15 or 16 stone. He always ran with his knees up, he was so powerful he scattered his opposite players so easily. [Another recruit at this time was] Kia Rika another centre threequarter.[11]

Now Kia Rika's grandson is in this country, as far as I know, currently playing rugby union for Cleckheaton. Then there were two others, the McDonald brothers, they were signed and [another] player was the famous George Nepia, supposedly the finest full-back ever to grace either code, rugby league or rugby union. He used to kick goals, never took a run, he just placed the ball down and swung his leg, a very powerful man indeed.

As I say that would be about 1937 and in the 1937–38 season they were so powerful they should have won the cup. They drew the first round, won the replay, drew the second round, won the replay, drew the third round, won the replay and they were drawing the semi-final right up till the final kick of the match against Barrow at Huddersfield, Fartown, two points each. The Barrow stand-off half, he was a well known player, he got the ball from a scrum on the halfway line, dropped a goal and they beat Halifax by the drop-goal. It was always said that he didn't drop the goal, he kicked it out of his hand and the referee hadn't seen him.

But, more than that, it was said that Halifax had so much money on bets that they would draw every round up until Wembley that they were trying to achieve that, and fell short on doing it. The following year with much the same team they steamrolled everybody.
Ronnie Wolfenden

Tha's sat in my seat!
They were wonderful days. I can remember them as clearly as anything and the spectators were always the same. It was curious, my uncle, he had a season ticket and we went on the stand at Parkside, in the centre stand. There weren't chairs or anything like that just forms. No numbers or anything. But he always sat in exactly the same spot and that applied to everybody.

One day there was an argument behind us. I can remember it as clearly as anything, because one of the people involved in the argument was the father of the Hunslet loose-forward, Harry Beverly

---

[11] Rika did not sign from Streatham & Mitcham

who went on the 1936 tour. Mr Beverley said, "Tha's sat in my seat" and this chap said "What do you mean, sat in your seat?" He said "I always sit there." He said "It's only a [bench] sit there". He said "No, that's where I sit!" and everyone around him, I remember, was saying "Yeah, that's his seat" and this fellow had to move. It was only a form.

When I became secretary, I put white marks on them and put numbers on. But in those days there weren't any and everyone was aggrieved at this poor fellow who come and inadvertently sat in Mr Beverley's seat. So, it was like that, and you could walk around the ground at Parkside and people were standing in exactly the same place every week and nobody took their places. So it was a way of life, you see.
Harry Jepson

Looking through the railings
So I used to go down and watch Rovers. I was only young. I can remember they played in all white. I can remember a fella called Sid Denton and [another called] Jim Denton. They used to lose more that they won. But before that, they did have a decent team, because they had some good forwards. Have you heard of Hunslet's terrible six? Well two of them were from Featherstone. We used to look through the railings. It wasn't very much to go in. But we used to get some decent teams down here. I can remember Jim Sullivan and Featherstone used to have a centre called Jack Hirst. He was marvellous. But the only thing was he had a bad knee. They always said that if he hadn't been crippled, he'd have been a world beater.
Jackie Blackburn

Watching the wartime stars
My heroes during the war were prop forward Harry Hammond, scrum half Harry Royal, and a stand-off called Tom Kenny. Loose-forward Charlie Seeling also of course, he stayed on and played a number of years at Dewsbury. He lived just below us in his later life and used to train every day as an old man running around the field at Crown Flatt. He was an athlete right into his latter days. He was a New Zealander, his father was the great international Charlie Seeling. It was tough was wartime rugby. I was a young kid so I saw them as massive anyway.

But looking at old photographs confirms they were big men, maybe not as fit as the modern chaps, and certainly not as athletic or as fast. But it was a completely different game then and I'm sure that the stars of that day would have fitted into today's game. They would have had all the benefits of modern diets and training. Personally, I think in a lot of respects it was more skilful. You got different sizes of player and the small guys would nip round the blind side and side-step and short kick. It was certainly different. The modern game and I'm not knocking it in any way isn't the game I was brought up with.

I remember Jim Sullivan, he was the biggest name playing and he played quite a few games for Dewsbury. He was a star and I was introduced to him. Again [he was] a big man and I remember watching him in training kicking at goal.

The ball was different in those days, it was heavier and he could kick it prodigious distances. He was quite a nice chap as well and played full-back. I remember Gus Risman playing in the centre to Alan Edwards who played on the wing. Alan later went onto play for Bradford Northern and had a lot of success. He was very fast.

Roy Francis was my favourite, when he guested for Dewsbury. He used to come for a cup of tea at our house which was next to the ground. Another smashing fellow, he was one of the few coloured people playing in those days. When I saw him, he was on the wing but he did play in the centre and other positions. Barney Hudson captained the side, having come to play from Salford, with Gus Risman. He was part of the great Salford side from before the War.

Vic Hey the Australian international also came to play at Crown Flatt as well. He stayed on and was coach for quite a while. He was born in Dewsbury before his family emigrated to Australia. Short and stocky, I remember seeing him play at Mount Pleasant. Batley had Bill Hudson playing for them, he had been a winger, but was now a forward and they had one ding-dong of a struggle that day. Bill Hudson knocked Vic Hey out and the sponge man came on as Vic Hey was coming round. The sponge man had a trilby hat on and Vic threw a punch thinking it was Bill knocking this hat off and nearly his head.

It was a hard game in those days, but it was not a dirty game. As semi professionals they played for winning pay. The winning pay bonus was paramount and they would do all sorts of things to achieve it. They played within the rules, but there was an element of ruthlessness in it. Today's game is hard, but the discipline is a lot better than it was in those days. Then, more players took the early bath. As a kid I used to sit on a wall watching the spectators on match day come and go. It always appeared to me then that they were excited going in and if they'd lost they were dejected and it was all quiet. But if they'd won, people stayed on and would go in the bar and two hours later you would see people staggering up the road. It was wartime and I spent a few nights in a big air raid shelter built in the Crown Flatt car park next to the ground.
Harry Waring

1945 to 1970

Conkers, string and cigarette cards
Rugby league had just started again and this was the first season immediately following the war. I was 10 at the time and loved the game. It was coincidental that my address at that time was 'Number 6,

/ 30 Featherstone, so it used to be interesting when it used to be the derby games, you know in the workshops there was a lot of stick flying about.

[At Post Office Road] there used to be an old big wooden main stand at the time and I know from when I was playing, the changing rooms were underneath the stand and you always knew if there was a big crowd because there was a buzz. You could hear 'em going up and down the steps and there was a really big buzz. The atmosphere used to be electric.

Keith Bell

1970 to 1995

Watching to learn
[As a player] you watch and you learn. I used to go to Cas and I used to go to Wakefield, I used to go all over to watch and you're "Why's he doing that?" You know what I mean, like Bobby Moore at football, "Why's he got all that time?" and you see it. [When I was a pro] I used to watch Malcolm Reilly a lot.

Mick Morgan

Jewish sports fans and rugby
Rugby, from a playing viewpoint, was very minority as far as the Jewish base was concerned, because it's a very hard game to play and the race in general are not rough and tumble people. I am, but that's just the way I am. Most Jewish people are not, they're much more head in a book.

There always have been Jewish rugby supporters. I'm sure there always will be, but I think they're in the minority. Most people I know go and watch Leeds United, for some reason. But there's a tremendous administrative involvement. In the 1950s the Swinton chairman was a man called Barnet Manson who I believe worked at Manchester hospital and I think he was chairman of the Rugby League one season. There was another guy called Dr Harold Roebuck who was the chairman of [Liverpool City] when they were quite a respectable team and winning quite a lot of games. I believe that he went on to be chairman of the Rugby Football League, both Jewish men. In this city you've got Ronnie Teeman who was chairman of both Hunslet and Bramley and he had at least two or three Jewish directors at Bramley with him.

Bernard Shooman

A sense of loyalty
[Bramley], it's the first club I ever watched, it's a hometown club, we were never going to be hugely successful like Wigan, St Helens [or] Leeds but it was a case of, 'that's the team I saw first' and I developed

an affinity and affection for them. Even though I travelled away quite a lot when I was working, I always kept in touch with them and always got to watch them when I could. There's a sense of loyalty, like a lot of sporting passions it gets in your blood. Even today I spend an inordinate amount of time and money following Bramley home and away, albeit at a slightly lower level to where we were before.
Andy Coldrick

An easy target
[Abuse from spectators] – I don't think the religious part, the minority part or the ethnic part plays any great part in it. I think it's just a vehicle for them to vent their feelings at certain people and that's a readily accessible reason to do it. It's just accidental I think, it's just an easy thing to pick on. When I started refereeing I got another couple of Jewish lads interested in it, one who actually went on to be a touch judge at Wembley. One of his pals, Howard, they used to go out on Leeds and District games and referee. I didn't used to referee that much in those days because I was doing senior football. I remember once there was a tough game, they asked me to go and referee it and sent these two guys with me, so there were three of us of the faith. They used to get a lot of stick because they were small and dark, nobody knows I'm Jewish if I don't tell them. We went out and they were getting a little bit of abuse. I wasn't, but somebody who knew me said "Bloody hell, look they've brought the rabbi with them this morning".
Bernard Shooman

What we did in the old days
Look at what we had to do in the old days. Odsal Stadium, you used to strip at the top. You had to walk all the way down through the crowd and then at the end of the game you had to walk back all the way through them and I'm convinced there were 10 times more at the end of the game up there than when the game started. They used to come in, never been at the game, and have a go at you. Honestly, it was 'bent this' and 'bent that' 'Thompson when are you going to retire?'

There was a lad, only me and him know this. He always used to stand at the top and block the thing when I was going in, and he was covered in the colours and he used to give me a load of hassle. I just said to him "I just want you to be here, my last match here". "What, what, what will you do then?" I said "You'll be first bounce in the bottom you." Guess what? My last match at Odsal, he wasn't there. To me sport is fun and I always had a sense of humour.

When you went to Warrington, at the car park I said to the bloke on the gate, "Referee", "Oh aye, park your car over there, you see that board there." It said on it "Reserved for the referee." I said "I'd rather not park my car there if you don't mind." He says "Why? What's

Billy Thompson awarding a try. (Courtesy *Rugby League Journal*)

up with parking it there?" I said "Well, you park yours there, I'll park in my old spot." I said "If they're gonna get you after the match they're gonna come looking. Not gonna tell them where I am."

You've got to have a bit of a sense of humour. It was a little bit hard at times you know, because there were one or two irate spectators, but you've got to laugh it off. When we talk about getting paid, I did three Wembley cup finals, I got £15 for the first one, that was 1971. I stayed at the County Hotel on Russell Square. They paid for me, I had a double room for me and my wife, they charged my wife for a single room, charged her for a meal in the hotel on the evening and a pound for a meal at Wembley Stadium. I can show you that in black and white. In 1978 there were 96,000 at Wembley, Leeds and St Helens, £20 I got. That was a good game. Three Wembley cup finals for me, and that was the only one I could say what a game that was. If Noonan had taken the ball in the last minute they [St Helens] could have scored and won the match, it was a brilliant game. I probably would have done it for nothing. But you wouldn't tell them otherwise that's what they would have paid you.

I'd refereed a test match at Wembley between Australia and Great Britain. This is what we had to do in those days, it's different now, it had to change. The teams were down there nearly a week in London training, I had to get up at five o'clock in the morning and I had to drive down to Wembley Stadium on the day of the match. After the game I had to come straight back. That was an international at Wembley. You had to run around for the test match. No overnight accommodation or anything, you just had to do it.

Billy Thompson

Strange places and strange things!

They were getting worse and worse and worse, not better and better and better. The more I watched them, the worse they got, but I still supported and went to watch Fartown. Me and a few mates would go to matches all over the place, can't even remember all the places we've been to. Strange places and strange things that we've done because somebody's decided they wanted to start a rugby league team there.

Nottingham. We went to Nottingham, the Harvey Haddon stadium. I run a taxi firm and we had a minibus. There were only two or three of us in the bus and as we were going down the M1 there was a coach on the side and it was the players. Luckily we were only a couple of miles from the junction for Nottingham so we threw six of them in the back of the bus, took them to the stadium, came back for another six or seven of them. Of course when we got to the stadium they suddenly said "Where's the kit?" so we doubled back. The least we were expecting was free entry, but some Nottingham official said "We can't afford it". I said "If it hadn't been for us you wouldn't have had a bloody match!" But that didn't matter so we still had to pay to get in.

We trailed to Carlisle once when Alex Murphy was coach. Carlisle, it's only two and a half hours out of your Sunday getting there. When we got there the pitch was half frozen and the Carlisle players were stripped, they wanted to play, but there was no way Murphy was going to play. It was too cold for him to stand at the side of the bloody touchline and watch that lot. They called the match off five minutes before it was due to kick-off. So we trailed all the way back from Carlisle for no reason.

Went to London, oh London, why they ever let them into rugby league? I don't know. It was alright when they played at Barnet because Barnet is North London, but then when they played at Crystal Palace, it was three hours to the end of the M1, four hours across bloody London. We were playing at Crystal Palace once, got stuck behind this car, Huddersfield car, Alex Murphy was in it, lost. We'd been before and so we ended up showing him how to get to the ground, of course once again they wouldn't have bloody played.

Literally been all over the place, Wales, places you have never even bloody heard of, Highfield. Highfield is a place outside St Helens. They original started as Liverpool Stanley, went to Liverpool City then became Huyton. I remember going to watch them at Huyton and Huyton is not one of the most well-off places. They never did owt in rugby league, always at the bottom and an average crowd attendance of about 300. When Fartown went to play that would go up to 650. It was a rundown place, we used to park the car, I remember saying to these two kids "Look after the car, there's a fiver here. If it's still here when we come back I'll give you another fiver." Sure enough, after the match these kids were stood by this car, they hadn't let anybody near it because they knew they were going to get a fiver for it.

The ground was falling to bits. You get dugouts at some clubs for [the coaches and subs] to sit in. They used to put two wooden benches out and I remember some kids walking on and pinching the bench. So the Huyton team couldn't sit down anywhere, they were sat on the grass watching the bloody game. You came away, if you didn't beat Huyton it was the lowest of the low and we just managed to win something like 19–18 so we were happy.

I remember going to Southend. Southend on a Friday night, Trevor Leathley scored his 100th try and I'll tell you what the crowd was: 85! There was a crowd of 85. Once again Fartown were probably about third from bottom, only Southend and probably Huyton below them. They played Southend on a Friday night. The traffic now is bad, but getting to Southend on a Friday night and the gaffer wouldn't give me time off. I was working for a coach firm at the time, and he said "You can leave at dinner time". I left at dinner time and I was in a little blue R reg Mini. I drove it all the way to Southend and watched this match, 85 people. We won, didn't matter, we'd won 24–16. Leathley got his 100th career try and then I drove back. I got back home at three o'clock in the bloody morning, had to be at work at six o'clock the following morning.

John Beaumont

Snowbound in Widnes
We played Warrington in 1990, it was Regal Trophy week and it snowed and snowed and snowed. We met at the Archie Gordon half past eight and my dad came down with us. We met up with the City boys, "Is the game going to be on?" We phoned Warrington and it was fine. We murdered Warrington 40 odd whatever and I said to my dad, who'd followed the coach over, let's go to Widnes to watch Leeds. So we left Warrington, me my dad and a friend, and went to Naughton Park. It was the probably the coldest game of rugby I've ever been to. How the game went ahead I do not know.

There was a tannoy announcement for my dad. My mum had phoned up the ground to tell us that the motorway had been closed, the M62, and we were stuck. So I've played rugby, I'm covered in mud, because the showers weren't the best where we'd played, we've been to watch Leeds in the Regal Trophy with about 150 other idiot Leeds fans, who obviously didn't have BBC, because the game was on and we're stuck. So my dad being my dad says "Let's go to the Chemic". So we got into the Chemic [pub] and it was like we're stuck here. We can't sleep in the car, it was cold and horrible.

Widnes isn't the nicest of places, is it? It's like a posh version of Shameless. So we're sat there and there was about eight or nine people in this pub. My dad's phoning up my mate's parents to say

"Your son's come to Widnes with us and we're stuck here and I'll look after him" and a bloke's come over. Only a young bloke and said "You're from Leeds aren't you, you're stuck here aren't you?" If I'd have been a bit older I'd have been thinking "He's going to rob us, he's already done us car over". He put his keys on the table and said "You can have my flat for the night, it's two bedrooms and I'll go and stay at my mum's." It was like: "But we don't know you and you don't know us at all." We're stuck 80 miles from home and he said "I've been to the game." That was what rugby league was, you know, it was freaky. If it hadn't been for him, who knows what would have happened.
Paul Kilbride

A sense of achievement
I think the best moment in refereeing to me wasn't a professional game, it was an amateur game and it was at Belle Isle [in Leeds]. Belle Isle in those days were a big rough team, with two or three ex-professionals. They could dish it out and they could play rugby. They were playing Milford, who were also doing very well then, but were not long on the road into the amateur game. They had a very strong team, again with some ex-professionals and they played in a local quarter-final at Belle Isle.

I heard whiffs from pals of mine that there were thousands of pounds in side bets going on what was going to happen and what wasn't going to happen, and he was going to see to him and so and so was going to see to someone else. There was a very big crowd and I went out and refereed it.

It was tough, but it was an excellent game, both sides played cracking rugby and it finished just about 18–16. Coming off I felt a great sense of achievement, people were coming up and saying "Well refereed, cracking game" and it really had been a superb game. That game was the best feeling I've ever had after a match. I didn't ask about the bets as they were nothing to do with me, but it was a tremendous game. No quarter asked and no quarter given, they were knocking spots off each other, but legally. That's the best game I've ever had. I think things like that happen to you in rugby league.

I had a Leeds and District match in South Leeds at Bisons' ground a couple of seasons ago... We were on the gate taking the money and there were lots of people coming in. We cashed up and were watching the match. A lady came across to me, about 40 something; she said "Are you Bernard? You don't know me but do you know my husband. That's him over there."

There was a big guy standing with a pipe leaning against the wall. "Oh yeah, I know him, used to play for [Dewsbury] Celtic". "Do you know him very well?" "I don't know him well, I refereed him. He's one of the lads, one of the players." "Well," she said "he's not a nice man, not a lot of people like him, he's not got a lot of time for most people. He's nasty, he really is, you have to be very careful with him. [But] when we came in today and you took our money he said to me, you couldn't wish to meet a nicer bloke than him. I just had to come and meet you because I've never heard him say that about anybody."

That's one of the things I look at in my career, it's great to hear things like that. It's not trophies or anything, just things that stick in your mind. I didn't know the lad, I knew him to referee and penalise but nothing else about him.

In the 1970s I refereed some Widnes matches, who were then coached by Vince Karalius. I didn't realise at the time, but we had something in common – our grandparents came from Lithuania.

Bernard Shooman

European Champions

Huddersfield are officially the European champions. You can't take that away from them until they have another competition. They got to the end of the season and they had arranged a tournament between two French sides and two English sides, one was Batley and one was Huddersfield. Batley refused to go because they weren't going to promise them any money for it, but Huddersfield thought it was a good idea for a holiday. So they went and they were supposed to play two games in France and one in Spain, but the two teams in France pulled out.

They ended up playing Treize Catalan, in the Olympic Stadium in Barcelona. Barcelona is the capital of the Catalan area and at the time they were either trying to create a record for the most number of sports in a stadium or show what sports the Catalan people play.

Of course because Treize Catalan was then a big team in French rugby league it was an obvious thing to do, play rugby league. Here you had Huddersfield playing Treize Catalan for the European Cup at the same time as some nutcase is chucking a bloody javelin across the field and shot-putters and horse riders, there was all sorts of sports. Because I run my own business, I couldn't just simply go around the south of France for a week and a half just on the off chance there was going to be a rugby match. I got a fella at the ground, Frank Doyle – the kit man, to ring me when they found out if they were gonna play. He rung me about the Friday to say "Yes we're definitely playing on Sunday, match in Barcelona, kicks off three o'clock."

This was May Day bank holiday so I rang round to see if I could find any flights, managed to get one from Manchester with British Airways which cost me £526 return, I wasn't gonna miss a match like that. My mate pulled out, said it was too much money for him. I flew, got a taxi to the Olympic Stadium, I had to leave with five minutes to go and at that point we were bloody losing. I only realised they won when I read the *Examiner* three days later. Got the taxi to catch my plane back to Manchester – that shows you what true supporters do!

There were a few Fartown fans there who had gone as part of a holiday. So they were looking at me as much to say "Well you weren't with us at the breakfast table this morning." There were other people who were watching this javelin throwing, there were other people who were watching the horses. The people who were throwing the javelin were thinking "What are them nutters doing on a rugby field?" To me as a Fartown fan this was important; this was the European Cup we were going to bloody win, the first trophy we'd won in years. It was surreal and then to come back and read about it in the *Examiner* made you think, yes it did happen. It was in a match report in the paper 'Huddersfield European Champions, Gary Senior scored a last minute try,' so it did happen.
John Beaumont

Going to Headingley together
You'd play rugby in the morning and you'd all go up to Headingley together. When I first started going I was next to the benches and then we had a phase of wanting to be in the South Stand near the spiral old staircase when I was about 14 or15. I used to go with my best friend Dean, who now plays and lives out in Australia. It was his family who originally got me into rugby.

So I remember going down the season they signed Andy Gregory, Andy Goodway, basically anyone over 30 … You could come to Leeds for right good jolly for a few years and you didn't have to drive a Lada, what they were about I'll never know. We used to have names for all the doylums in the crowd, wherever you stood there'd always be a doylum. There used to be 'Annoying man' and 'Fat sweaty man'. They'd be going absolutely crazy. We're 14 or15, these were 40 year old blokes, and it's like 'what are you doing?' Then, we moved from there when I was playing at Milford. We used to go with the lads and used to stand in the corner of the old scoreboard end. But the game was beginning to change before Super League. There were all the rumours that Wigan had gone full-time and Shaun Edwards was paid to sit in a hut and sign balls for kids and it was "I want a job like that".
Paul Kilbride

5. Stars and personalities

Before 1945

My father and Albert Rosenfeld
I always tell them this, and I'm sure if he's looking down now he'll say "are you still cracking that?" Albert Rosenfeld played on one wing and my father played on the other. They scored 85 tries between 'em in a season. Albert Rosenfeld scored 80 and my father scored five! It'll never be beaten that, 80 tries in season, my father got five. He weren't that good [my father]. But I've got a photograph... 1920 it was taken, in a claret and gold shirt.
Billy Thompson

Jonty Parkin
Everybody worked down the pit, even Jonty Parkin. Five pounds doesn't buy you much now, but in 1913 Jonty Parkin signed for Wakefield Trinity for five pounds. He started at Sharlston Intermediates [and] went on to be one of the most famous all-time great players. In fact he lived within 100 yards from where you're sat, in one of them houses over there. Wakefield signed him for a fiver. He bought a fishmonger's in Wakefield when he got famous. He was quite a good businessman. He went on three tours. He went in 1920, 1924 and 1928 and all the three tours he was carried out of that pub, [The Sharlston Arms] head high, shoulder-high by all the players who played at the time, into a waiting car and he was whisked off. "For he's a jolly good fellow" they used to sing. In 1946, when [Sharlston Rovers] played Workington [in the first round of the Challenge Cup] – it wasn't a lot of money – but he gave every player 50 pence. It might buy you five pints, it might buy you 10 pints in them days and he bought them a fish and chip supper. He was at the game.
Graham Chalkley

Ben Gronow, my grandfather
My grandfather was Ben Gronow, who joined the [Huddersfield] club in 1910 after coming up from Wales. He played for Bridgend rugby union and then went on to play four times for Wales in 1910. In fact he was the first man to kick off at Twickenham, against England. Unfortunately he kicked it straight to the English guy who scored.

He was stonemason when he signed for Huddersfield. I think the fee involved was about 120 gold sovereigns, which was a lot of money in those days. So he came up to Huddersfield, they gave him a trade and he played for Huddersfield for 18 to 20 years.[15]

---

[15] From 1910 to 1928

A bronze bust of Douglas Clark, who played for Huddersfield 485 times between 1909 and 1929 was unveiled at the Galpharm Stadium on 14 July 2010. From left: David Gronow (former Huddersfield RL Club Players Assoc secretary), Joyce Dempsey (Clark's niece), Ken Senior (chairman, HRLCPA), Rod Wright (secretary HRLCPA). (Courtesy David Gronow)

The thing I can remember about him was he had huge hands. He could hold a ball in one and pass it for yards and yards and yards. A gentle guy, but on the field I would imagine that when he got with Douglas Clark and one or two more of the Huddersfield pack, then that all changed. But I knew him as just a gentle man.

He toured twice, 1920 and 1924. He missed out on the 1914 tour because of injury or he'd have toured three times. But he made some good friendships over there and at the end of the last tour he was one of the first to go over [to play in Australia]. He emigrated in I think it was 1926 or 1927.

He went to play for Grenfeld in the Australian country and did quite well. I think they liked him over there and I think he was there for a couple of years. My family went with him. My father and my uncle Gwyn were only maybe two years old then. My uncle Sid was actually born over there. Then he came back, sort of resurrected his career a bit and then retired. But he brought over another good player, Ernie Mills, and he played for Fartown and was a prolific points scorer. [My grandfather played with] Wagstaff and Rosenfeld. I actually met Rosenfeld, another unassuming guy.

The other guy I can remember him introducing me to was Jonty Parkin. He toured with Parkin as well. It's just how you see them. I mean Rosenfeld was quite a small guy and I'm looking at it as a 10 or

11 year older. He scored 80 tries this guy, I mean at the time you don't think that he is the world record holder. At the time you don't realise, but thinking back it's marvellous. My granddad, they gave him life membership of the club, because of what he'd done for them. He served on the football committee as well. So I used to go on with him and my father, when my father finished playing. But my granddad would take me into the dressing room and he'd say hello to people. He was very well respected. My granddad would go in and he had a waist coat and shirt sleeves I remember a fob he had tucked in his pocket and it was one of his championship medals.
David Gronow

Frank Gallagher, Jimmy Ledgard and other Dewsbury players
I can still remember one loose-forward who was picked and went on tour and he played for Dewsbury, that was Frank Gallagher. That was in 1924 and he had a good tour. My recollection is we were playing Batley; they were a good side then. They came to the Crown Flatt and Gallagher should have been playing for Dewsbury. But during the week he had been transferred to Batley and he played for Batley instead. He was captain of Batley I think when they won the championship.

There's one of them I know very well and that's Jimmy Ledgard because his daughter and my daughter were mates. He played for England at full-back and he went on tour. I wouldn't say he was the best ever, but he was the best I've ever seen at catching a ball. You'd have thought he had suction on each of his fingers. He could put one hand over the touchline and, of course, if the ball goes over the touchline and doesn't hit the ground it's still in play, and he'd catch it if he got his fingers to it. He wasn't very fast as a runner, but he was a good kicker. He wasn't all that big – I don't know where he got the power – but it's the follow through. He's another player I don't think would ever get cautioned in his life.

We had one who played at Dewsbury, a good player, Marchant played loose-forward, and if somebody did something wrong against him his fists would come up. Nothing dirty about it, he was doing it all in the open. He used to get sent off regularly and in the end he couldn't play. He didn't hit anybody on the sly, he put his fists up "come on then".

He was a great player, Vic Hey. He played with Leeds and then he came to Dewsbury and was going back on such and such a boat to Australia. He'd finished with Dewsbury; we'd given him a gold watch. But the boat was cancelled so he played two or three games for Hunslet before he went back. I think he was the best player I've seen taking him all the way around. He was a stand-off half, he could run he was strong and big enough to either knock them out of the way or beat them gently. He was about 13 or 14 stone without being fat:

great shoulders, body strength and he could still run, give a dummy. He'd one fault, if anything, and that was when the other side got the ball and the scrum-half was passing to the stand-off he measured it and tried to get to the stand-off to tackle him at the same time as the ball. Of course 14 stone coming at you, and you were catching the ball, you had no defence, and down he went. Just occasionally he got there too soon and that's an offence of course.

Morris and Harry Child

Cyril Halliday

Fred: Hooker, [my father, Cyril] he only ever played hooker.

Peter: Up until the 1980s he held the record for the most consecutive appearances. Keith Elwell took it over, Widnes player. But for years and years my grandfather held the record. It was something like 300 appearances.

Fred: He never missed a game through injury or owt like that. The first time he went in to hospital it was in his 80th year. He was a right keep fit fanatic. He used to have a cold shower every morning and he did Yoga every day.

Peter: He had his potassium broth. He was signed from Elland by Halifax.

Fred: He played for Elland Wanderers as they called them then.

Peter: He transferred from Halifax to Huddersfield in about 1930.

Fred: He started when he was 16 and he played up until the War started. He was still in't first team at Keighley.

Peter and Fred Halliday

Ken Jubb

They lost it [the 1938 Championship Final] the week before.[16] Do you know what with? Leeds had two great forwards sent off. There were three that got sent off, two Leeds men and a Wigan man. They were fighting like hell. He sent all three of them off. Watson he was a second-row forward with Jubby, a big pal of Jubby's. When he got back, Jubby, he was at this side of the field opposite the clock, and when he walked off his wife met him and hit him with her handbag. She went for him. "You big silly bugger", she shouted out. She knew he'd be out for the week after. She hit him with her handbag.

Oh he was a good 'un. In fact I'd put him as the best forward I've seen. That's my opinion and with Clues and all – Ken Jubb. He used to have his party piece. He'd get the ball and sway a bit and as he went a bit down the field he'd give it such a boot up in the air, race straight over and finish underneath it. It was his party piece. They used to say

---

[16] In fact, Leeds played Wigan on 16 April and won 21–9. The Championship Final, which they lost 8–2 to Hunslet, was on 30 April.

that. He stopped some years with Leeds, he came in about 1933 and stopped while 1947.
Stanley Pickles

Charlie Seeling and 'Plonk' Rhodes
I'll sing you a little song, that was handed out on paper, to the tune of *Daisy.*
"Dewsbury, Dewsbury, give us a victory do
We want Vasey to score a try or two
It must be a real team feeling
You must feed Gill and Seeling
And you can win, play with a whim and Wembley mood today"

The thing about Charlie Seeling – his father played for Wigan too – and he lived near the Dewsbury ground. He got a pub at Dewsbury Moor and we'd been to Odsal and we called in his pub on the way back. Of course he was behind the bar and naturally we got talking about rugby. We talked about one of the Dewsbury forwards, Plonk Rhodes. I said "Plonk Rhodes, he was a tough bloke, but he was clean, he never did a wrong action." He said "Oh didn't he?"

We'd been talking about when Dewsbury went to Wembley and in the third round they went to Warrington and won... Warrington were a far better team than Dewsbury. Dewsbury had good forwards, but Warrington were a class side. Charlie Seeling was playing for Warrington and that day he said, "This clean player you are talking about, Plonk Rhodes, the ball was kicked over the Dewsbury line and I was about to drop on it and a hand came out and the word was 'Yarked', got [me] by the collar and pulled [me] back. Didn't hurt me and they got a penalty, but I should have scored. It was a wrong action." Charlie would have been about 19 then, came to Dewsbury in his latter days and finished off playing with Dewsbury.
Morris and Harry Child

Eric Harris
His skill was his elusiveness. He wasn't as fast as Smithy [Stan Smith] and [Drew] Turnbull and people like that. He could use his cleverness and his skill. We were at Headingley one night and they were playing Swinton in the top four knock out and Swinton got a goal just before half-time, it was 2–0. Eric Harris got Leeds only try that night. Under the posts and they kicked the goal and won 5–2. There was only about five minutes to go. They were attacking were Swinton on the Leeds '25' and they threw a long pass out to the wing man who was unmarked; never thinking Eric Harris would run onto it. A big yell went up, you've never heard a yell like it. A big yell all over the ground because Eric Harris, straight in he was, off down the field and he beat man after man. Then there was only the full-back to beat and the fella

said "How he beat me, how he got by me I shall never know." He said "I had him! but he wasn't there." So he was a very clever fella, they couldn't stop him. They were frightened to death of him. He was there 10 years and in that time he got nearly 400 tries, which was remarkable. He was a great wingman. In fact I would say for smartness and that, he took some beating.
Stanley Pickles

Gus Risman
The game was littered with stars. The best player I ever saw was Gus Risman. He was a marvellous player and had it not been for the war, he would probably have been even greater. He lost six years like so many players and in other sports, like [Len] Hutton.

We now have, in rugby league, a scholarship scheme. Well Lance Todd, who was manager of Salford in the 1930s, he virtually had a scholarship scheme. He used to sign players on – young players from South Wales and Gus Risman came from South Wales. He took them to Salford and found them somewhere to live often together, well chosen lodgings where the lady of the house would look after them, and sometimes get them a job on the ground staff. They played rugby league for Salford and he got a great side together. So stars were groomed all over the place. The half-back pair for Salford, Watkins and Jenkins, they were wonderful players. Every team had at least one star. Batley, I can remember at Batley there used to be a feller called Bill Riches, he was a great centre for Batley. He never toured Australia, but he [joined] Hull.
Harry Jepson

A Tale of two Sullys
It was a long time ago now, but whenever I was asked if I had played rugby with anybody famous, I would relate that I had passed the ball to the immortal Jim Sullivan on the halfway line who ran and scored a try without a hand being laid on him. The reality was that I was only eight years old at the time. I lived just over the wall from Dewsbury's Crown Flatt and in my Dewsbury shirt used to go and see my heroes arrive at the ground a couple of hours before a match. It was the war time super team era of Eddie Waring's guest players and Mr Sullivan (who didn't call adults 'Mr' in those days?) was out on the ground already in his playing strip stretching his legs. He asked me to help him with his training by standing on the halfway line and passing the ball to him as he ran past me. This was my hero who had asked me to play in his two man team, it was my Wembley. He took the pass, side stepped a couple of imaginary players as well as the groundsman who was marking the try line and scored under the posts. The super star then picked up the ball, ran at speed and placed the ball on the centre spot with the points facing toward the touch lines

and continued running to the other posts. He turned, ran toward the ball and without stopping converted the try he had scored. The ball went through the middle and landed on the terracing behind the goal. I don't remember anything about that day's match, but in my mind's eye I still see the big man kicking that ball what must have been over 60 yards.

Some years later, our school team played a Saturday morning game shortly after the Easter break. Another Sully, Mick, had played for our school, but as he had left that Easter wasn't eligible and was watching the match. Because our opponents had turned up with only 12 players we were some 40 points up at half-time and some bright Herbert, our sports master if my memory serves me correctly, suggested that Mick play the second half for our opponents to make a game of it. Mick was then a slim raw boned athlete with genuine speed, but more than that he was fearless with a very high pain threshold. As they say, he could take it as well as give it. Mick played that second half, and playing full-back I had the doubtful privilege of trying to stop him on numerous occasions. We lost by some 20 points, all scored by Mick. Leaving the field black and blue, I didn't know if I had been drilled, bored or countersunk. That afternoon and having to cry off through injury, I watched our Shaw Cross Boys Club team and saw Mick score a couple of tries and save more with his ferocious tackling. This Sully, like Jim, became a legend representing his clubs and country with honour and created try scoring and appearance records yet to be beaten some 50 years on.

It was heartening to read in the *Rugby League Journal* that Mick has been inducted as a "Rugby League Heritage Legend", an honour he justly deserves. Jim Sullivan became posthumously a member of the Hall of Fame in 1988. I hope that when Mick is inevitably honoured he doesn't suffer the same fate.
Harry Waring

1945 to 1970

Tommy McCue
I've always praised Tommy McCue. Tommy had been [on the Lions' tour to Australia] in 1936, Gus had been there in 1932 and 1936, and these two formed this, like, company of pals and it went right through the tour. I mean there was no coaches, no trainers. If you were training, Tommy McCue would just say, "Do it this way". You know, you learnt as you went along and it was marvellous, really, to experience it. We trained everyday on the ship. It was such a good flight deck, and we'd train and it was great help really.

Risman and McCue installed in us that when you got there you had to be fit. You know, you had to start off well and everybody had to be on top form. They encouraged this. McCue was magical... When we got there, Tommy was a little stubby chap with a bald head and he's the last on the photo because he's the smallest. They said "They're bringing an old man here." He was pretty tough, Tommy and he said "I'll bloody show 'em if I'm an old man or not". He made tries. He made people play well. I mean, he made Ike Owens a star. He made Willie Davies and Willie Horne, at stand-off, such great players. He made wingers, I mean, wingers going in for three tries and he's passed the ball that's given the try. A brilliant player he was, and to me, who was younger, you kind of idolised him. He was that good.

If I could visualise something, it's Tommy McCue coming from a scrum in the middle of the field and giving a back pass to Ike Owens and Ike shooting up the middle of the field. He used to run with a, like, Kangaroo style run. Superb!

Bryn Knowelden

Brian Bevan

If we're talking wing men, I must talk about Brian Bevan, because what Bevan did was impossible. I've been on the terraces and watched him score and turned around to the chap next to me and said "What we've just seen is beyond the realms of human possibility." I wrote a little bit about him Robert Gate's book, *The Great Bev*.

In his early days, he came over to Warrington and played trials in the 'A' team. Bill Shankland was apparently a friend of Bev's father. Bill Shankland had played for Warrington. He'd come to Leeds and was golf professional at Temple Newsam. He played in the Ryder Cup did Bill, and Bev's dad had apparently told him "My son's coming over, he wants a game of rugby. Can you fix him up?" So he recommended him, I gather, to Hunslet and Leeds, neither of which club pursued him and it's understandable. It's just after the War, there's a state of flux everywhere and you're getting recommendations. They didn't pursue it. The story goes that he turned up and they rejected him on appearance. But I don't think he ever went to either club.

So Bill recommended him to Warrington and he played a couple of 'A' team games before he went back to Australia for demob. Warrington were very impressed by his trial games apparently, and of course signed him and brought him back again. I remember him in his early days. He'd catch the ball with a phalanx of the opposition within touching distance of him and turn around and run towards his own line, like a man gone mad, and because of his superior pace he'd open a 20 yard gap. Then he'd turn and face the opposition. "Right I've got the ball and I've got space, here we go," bump, bump, bump, bump. The only parallel I can make with him was Charlie Chaplin or Buster Keaton in the silent film days, running through the whole of the New York police force, dib dib dib dib dib dib.

I've literally seen what appeared to be 13 prostrate bodies on the field when Bev put the ball down. It probably wasn't, but it looked like it, because he would literally go through the whole team. With the ball in hand, he's the fastest I've seen without a clock to record times. If you talk about, is he the fastest on the clock, well he probably wasn't. Berwyn Jones must have been close to being so and he performed a feat that staggered me.

He was playing for Wakefield, and there was a try on for Wakefield who were playing Hull. As the ball was passed to Berwyn it was intercepted by Clive Sullivan and he was no slouch. Berwyn has to turn round and chase him and [Sullivan had] about 20 yards start and he caught him. Now you'd say that's impossible. But I saw it. It happened and that made me think "Is this fellow faster than Bevan?"

But match after match Bevan was just showing what he could do. He played against Leigh once without scoring and a wingman named [Albert] 'Nebby' Cleworth, a little lad that was known for little else, but that he stopped Bevan. But when Bevan played Leigh in the return match he scored seven. Seven tries! That was the highest he ever scored. He never got more than that. But you talk these days about scoring a century of tries. Bevan scored a century of hat tricks. What I say about Bevan, he was the most under-rated player that's ever played, simply because no one knew how good he was. You just couldn't appreciate how good he was. He was the greatest.

On a Saturday night after we'd all played our matches, various teams coming back to Warrington, I'm coming from Oldham, the Widnes lads are coming in, and we used to drop in at Harry Bath's pub, the Britannia. Bev was, a couple of times, in there. Warrington had obviously come and had a few drinks and dispersed and Bev was on his own moaning to me about "Where's the team spirit", and so I would run him home. He hadn't got a car. I would run him home to Winock where he lived and he'd show me his sprinting cups and whatever.

He wasn't a freak, he was a very great athlete, totally without ego. I asked him to come with me to youth club that Cyril Smith was running in Rochdale, in my Rochdale days. Cyril Smith became MP, and he asked me to find a personality. I asked Bev – would he come along to this youth club. I had a Ford Popular, my first post-war car, unheated, Bev hadn't got a car. I drove him from Warrington along the East Lancashire road, shrouded in mist, unheated car. He spent a couple of hours at this youth club, talking to anybody who wanted to talk to him, signing autographs, no side whatsoever, same on the return journey. No payment ever thought about, and that was Bev. I think his wife was upset that he didn't make out of rugby what he ought to have done. And she's perfectly entitled to feel that, because what would Bevan make today? He'd be a millionaire.

I think possibly his illness may have been showing a little bit, because he wasn't freakish looking in his early days. You wouldn't say he had a mop of hair, like his brother Owen Bevan, who came to

Warrington. But he had hair, and he was phenomenally strong in the body. I mean he'd go into tackles and twist out of them.
Joe Warham

Frank 'Dolly' Dawson and the Halifax side of the 1950s

We were fortunate that Stan [Kielty] and I came together just at the time Halifax started some good buying. The main chap that I always said changed Halifax no end was Les White, a top second-row forward from Wigan, who toured about twice to Australia. He was a crack player. He was on his last legs, but he came and changed our pack. At that time Jack Wilkinson started as a lad of 18 and we got Thorley. Ackerlay had always been there, but that front-row lasted us for about six or seven seasons. It was a wonderful front row. They signed Ken Trail, loose-forward.

Second-row we had Albert Fearnley, who was a nutter! He was a lovely chap. But as a player, I've never met anybody as dedicated. When Albert went on, he went on to win. Loosing didn't come into it at all. There was Fearnley and Schofield and Henderson came we always had a really good pack of forwards and Stan and I started ticking behind it. Dolly [Dawson] came about that time as well, about 1951 or 1952 and he was respected. I wouldn't say he was a good coach. He had his own way and he was a character. He was a hard man. You did it and if you didn't you got thrown out. But if you were doing well for him he looked after you. Funnily enough he wasn't a man who was teaching you how to play clever rugby. He'd train us for fitness and that and then he used to throw the ball to either Stan or myself and say "Take all the backs and do your moves".

Stan was the clever man as regards moves, and we used to coach ourselves... crisscrossing and all that. We used to practice to move the ball to open a gap and somebody was through it. We were quite a good defensive side, Halifax, but not everyone liked our style of play. But we could turn it on when we got on top. There were some sides, where the packs were unbelievable, like the Hull pack. You knew before you went out.

Instructions from Dolly were "Right, Thorley, Coverdale, give him one". Tommy Harris were the hooker so "Ackerley, smack him one". And that were Dolly's bit of football. He was quite a character, but he was successful. All the forwards used to have to fight. If you didn't fight you didn't get in for Dolly. We got one lovely player from Rochdale, Derek Schofield. A proper gentleman, you know. He was a manager in a mill and was that bit above most of the common lads, you know. But a nice chap was Derek. But he wouldn't hurt anybody. If you didn't hit anybody Dolly used to go mad. He was comical. But you needed some good forwards or hard forwards in those days. There were some good teams about.
Ken Dean

Clive Sullivan

I remember once competing in 1966 at Jedburgh. They all wrapped round festivals and fairs and gatherings like all the common riding events in Scotland. It was Jedburgh border games. I hitchhiked up there and Clive Sullivan gave me a lift back down. He'd just nicely signed for Hull about a year earlier. He was still a semi-unknown if you like. But he said he was competing in these events to get himself a bit fitter. He said "My ambition is to hit it high in rugby league," and he did do. There was Clive and his brother Brian who also competed and another guy who brought the car up and they gave us a lift down. He competed in quite a few sprint events and did well in them and all and his brother Brian did as well.

Quite a lot of years later, it was well into the 1980s, only about a month before he died. He was down at Wembley and he made a beeline for us. I thought that was brilliant. We had a picture took. I didn't know he had only a matter of weeks to live at that time. We've got a right nice picture somewhere in the family album, me and my older lad and his mate and Clive's got his arms around them. There's Neil Kinnock signing autographs in the background. It should have been the other way round.

Roger Ingham

1970 to 1995

Malcolm Reilly

We worked together, me and Malcolm, at South Yorkshire Motors at Pontefract. I was in the stores Malcolm was a mechanic, a very poor one! Well a fitter actually. We used to take the mickey out of him because he was a footballer. There was me, a lad called Dave Garbutt who played for Keighley, and Vaughan Thomas, who played for Featherstone at Wembley in 1967. He was a salesman.

Reilly was a fitter and he used to come to the stores for things and this day he came and he was chuffed to death. He said the football team didn't turn up and they were short on the rugby pitch. He'd played and scored two tries. The following week he came and said "Bramley want to sign me on". He'd only played twice so whoever the scout was from Bramley, he must have been a genius! Within a week or two Cas came and he signed and the rest is history.

He'd played six games for Kippax when Cas signed him. We used to have a few battles after that. He was a competitor. You knew you were playing. He was a good footballer as well.

Mick Morgan

Albert Fearnley

Albert Fearnley always used to say to me, "Big Jim Mills, you can't hurt him because he's too big, he's six feet four [inches]. When he's hitting

123

you, just keep getting up and laughing at him. Laugh at him, smile at him, ask 'do you want the ball Jim?'" and that's what you used to do.

Albert would say to me "I've been on the other side of the coin, I've been the man giving it to players like you, and when they laugh at you and offer you the ball, it's so infuriating, you want to kill them and then you lose." That's what I used to do; try and make them look stupid. Albert used to say to me "Try and make them look stupid, the big lads who are giving you some stick."

Albert was a winner and from day one I used to think to myself "I'm glad I never played when he played" because he had a hell of a reputation. He always used to say to me "You reckon that you had the hardest pack in the game at Hull in the 50s? No we did at Halifax." He said "The Drake twins, Johnny Whiteley, Mick Scott and all them at The Boulevard, they were nothing. There was me, Les Pearce...", and all these, I'd never even heard of half of these guys. Then he said "We used to always tame that Boulevard six."

But I had that much respect for Albert I ended up playing under his command at three different clubs. I played for four different clubs, but three of them I played under Albert. He was the guy that gave me my first coaching opportunity at Blackpool Borough.

I've [generally] got nothing but good memories of Albert, but the one bad memory I have was when I was expecting to get the nod for the 1973 Cup Final against Featherstone at Wembley and he gave the nod to Barry Seaborne. Now I'm not saying I was a better scrum-half than Barry Seaborne because he played in all the cup rounds prior to the final against Featherstone. But in the semi-final against Castleford at Headingley he broke two ribs. From the semi to the final there were about five weeks in between and there were about seven league matches to play to bring us up to the end of the season and then the final. I played in all those seven league matches and I was told by the physio and the club doctor that no way would Barry Seaborne be fit to play in the final, and Albert gambled.

He told me two days before the final, when I thought I was going to be playing. He said "I'm gonna give him the nod". He said "I think he has got greater experience than you, he has played here before, he's played in Australia, he's played for Great Britain, he's done this that and the other." I said "I'm not disputing any of that Albert, but in my own defence, I'm just going to say this and I don't think it's going to wash with you. He's not fit and I think he might let you down." Anyway, he played him and Barry will be the first to admit he should never have played. But there you go. Had it been me I would have done exactly the same. If I'd have got the nod for a final and I wasn't fit I think, at that time, I'd have played.

When I was coaching in later years, I did things that weren't popular with players, but you do what you think is right at the time

and that's all Albert did, you know, he did what he thought was right at the time and it backfired on him.
Bak Diabira

Characters from the 1970s
It's the talking that does it. Fists fly at rugby, they always will do. It's a physical game and if you get a tap, I used to walk behind them sometimes and say, "You've just given him one, in 10 minutes he's gonna give you one. That's the end then!" It usually finishes at that, they see sense then. Elbows they're in the dressing room straight away, you don't mess about with them.

Up front and scrums and getting down you'd give them a bit of leeway. In the old days, they used to say "It's our head" and a big hand used to come out and said "It's yours if you can get it". The first scrum usually erupted in a brawl because everyone missed the space and the band played *Happy days are here again*. We used to have bands in my day, can you remember that?

[There were players] like Kevin Ashcroft the hooker, you know what I mean. "Back the five yards, Kevin, back to me I'll mark the five yards," "Hey Billy, if that's five yards, I wouldn't want [you] to fit me a carpet." "It's a penalty now, because I wouldn't want [you] to fit me one." Get on with the job you see.

We had a rapport. Dennis Hartley, flipping heck, do you know I've never seen Dennis Hartley have any attention at all, but anybody that came into contact with him, they had to have it. You know what he once said to me? I said "Come here Dennis, you've just hit him, he wasn't even looking your way." "That's the time to hit him Billy" he said. What do you do after that? "Never mind Dennis, bear it in mind". Jim Mills, big Jim, the assassin from the Rhonda Valley. "What are you doing now Billy, I never touched the man?" I said "Well it's only me and you here and I haven't laid a finger on him and what's he doing on the floor?" "You get it like a game of tig and pass" he said. He was a big fella him.

You've got to have a go, they'll trust you, but you'll come across them you can't do owt with and it's the dressing room. You have your bad games, you know. You have games where you go home, and a good referee goes home and he thinks "Where did I wrong today?" "Never got hold of so and so early on" or something like that or "Should have sent them two off and given him another chance, spoilt the game". You learn by your mistakes you see.

When it flows, not when you end up blowing your whistle every two minutes, that's when you enjoy a game. You don't want to blow the flipping whistle. It happens some times, as I say, when you go home you sit down and think "where did it go wrong?"

You want it to be flowing, scrum down, ball goes in and they get it out and it goes again, but it doesn't happen all the time. Genuine mistake, but you tell the bloke 10 rows up in the terrace side. [The players] have a drink [after the match] and they might mention a few words that are unrepeatable, "But you're alright Billy". You do, have a drink with them and especially now when you go to some past players dinners and all that. Imagine that, being invited as a guest to a past players' reunion where they didn't want to know you!

That's a good thing in rugby league, the past players where they all turn up for their dinner and they all reminisce. They invite players from other clubs and they talk about old times. Talk about when they played, when they played at so-and-so and then they'll tell you their woes and how much money they drew for that. Some had some good money and some hadn't. Probably tell you about how much you cost them. I always put my hand in my pocket, "How much do I owe you?"

No, they are a great lot. It's a bit of fun and look back on your career, "Did you get it right all the time?" "No, definitely not". Lads that didn't really speak to you for a long time speak a bit now. You get in "Come on, let's have a pint." Having said all that, I'd come back tomorrow and go through the same again, because it's one hell of a game.
Billy Thompson

Dave Topliss
Me and Topper, God bless his soul. We used to do loads of moves on us own. I remember at Oldham the back end of his career when Frank Myler was the coach. Frank was a lovely man, but he was never going to be the best coach. Great players they just did it. So we used to organise things and get Terry Flanagan involved as well. Just take time out on your own at training sessions to organise these things. Two or three, that's all you needed, don't complicate it. You have your little ploys. Topper knew what I was going to do and if I see a photo of me in the Wakefield days or even Oldham days Topper's behind me. Topper came in the summer of '68 [to Wakefield]. He signed on as we came back from Wembley. That was the first time I saw Topper, his debut was on the wing at Halifax. Johnny Freeman was on the wing and Colin Dixon in the centre. He played on the wing and I played in the centre.
Mick Morgan

Tommy Smales
The best [coach] tactically I had while I was at Featherstone, and he took over in about 1975, was Tommy Smales, the scrum-half. He took Castleford to Wembley in 1970. Derek Turner took 'em the first year [1969] and Tommy took 'em the second. Tommy was absolutely fantastic, he was thinking all the time. You'd get a phone call, "I've been thinking about something". He had me out training in the pitch black doing things that he'd been thinking about. He first took over,

just before Christmas and on Christmas Day he phoned us up. We were playing Cas on Boxing Day, and he had the Travellers pub down the road, "Could I go down for 10 minutes" he had summat to show me. It was Christmas tea time and the wife wasn't right happy. So I said "It'll only be 10 minutes". He'd got Phil Butler, who was the scrum-half and set a table out in the middle of the gym – he had a gym upstairs we all used to use at the time. He had us doing a scrum move round a table. That 10 minutes turned out to be two and a half hours, until we got it right. We got back in about eight o' clock.

We beat Cas. It didn't come off that day, but after, we used to score every game from it. It was like a dummy run from the scrum-half, he'd run one way and the loose-forward would come round the other way. All the other teams started doing it and they called it 'Featherstone'. But it was move Tommy had done when he'd played with Dave Valentine at Huddersfield. It had been forgotten about.

Tommy was really good tactically, the football was unbelievable. He still helps a lot of players today. He's a physio now, he has players going to see him. When he had the pub up there it was like a who's who of rugby league. He'd have all the top players going for treatment on injuries and that and he'd take 'em on one-on-ones to the local park for speed work and trying out little things in their game. He'd do it all out of the good of his heart, out of interest in the game. He was a brilliant bloke. I think he's a Castleford bloke, but played originally his rugby at Featherstone. But at that time there were about five scrum-halves on the books at Featherstone that were all first team potential, so Tommy moved on to Huddersfield and then Bradford. He captained Great Britain as well.

But he had the local pub here for years and years and built a gym upstairs with a sauna and that. I mean that was before it's time, not a lot of players did weights at that time and Tommy got us doing some in his gym. He was the first one to do this match warm up before a game. He actually bought us all tracksuit tops himself. He used to take us out warming up before a game. Nobody had ever heard of it, crowd used to be taking the mickey and all sorts and then within a couple of years everybody's doing it. He played and coached in Australia did Tommy.

Keith Bell

Keith Bridges

Best ball-getter ever was Bridgie. We played in the World Cup against Australia at the SCG, Sydney Cricket Ground. We were getting beat 10–5 with about two or three minutes to go. The ball goes into touch about 20 yards from their line. I was playing prop that day, Mike Coulman's at eight, Bridgie's at nine. I remember going down and we said "we need this Bridgie." It was their head and feed and in those days the loose-forward could detach onto the short side. John Sattler's

detached onto the short side. Raudonikis was feeding the scrum, Johnny Lang was the number nine for Australia, Beetson was number eight, Randall number ten. Fed the scrum, Bridgie never struck. They've no loose-forward in, Raudonikis was about to pick it up and all of a sudden this great thing came and whoosh yanked it back and of course Nashy picked it up and Kenny Gill was on for the injured Roger Millward. So the loose-forward's on the short side, Raudonikis is thinking "what's gone on there?" All of a sudden Nashy's run across and dropped him inside and he's under the posts is Kenny Gill. So we drew 10 apiece in the World Cup. But all the press and everything was "what a move!" Gill and Nash got all the headlines, but me and Mike Coulman knew. Bridgie, he got that ball. That's what the press doesn't see. He'd no right to win that.
Mick Morgan

David Ward and other hookers in the 1970s
If you got, like, me and David Ward against each other, the referee knew what was going to happen. So what they'd do was at the first scrum down they'd pull us out and say "Right, cut this out" because they knew me and David had this thing about trying to beat each other. You did with most hookers, but because at that time David was a top hooker as well – they knew we were going try that bit harder. I remember one match, I think we both got sent off at Featherstone, and the referee just pulled us out and said just get off, because all we were doing was spoiling the game. But that's how intense it was in them days, the rivalry, hooker against hooker.

You played two games. You played a game of rugby and, even if you lost the match, if you beat the hooker, it was a big thing for you. Kevin Ashcroft, Graham Liptrot, Tony Karalius, Clive Dickinson, but Clive was older than me, there were loads of hookers in those days. Colin Clarke, who's Phil Clarke's father, he was one of the top hookers as well. There were so many. You couldn't go into a game with a bad hooker. Nowadays it wouldn't make a difference, because the ball is put into the second-row.
Keith Bridges

Mick O'Neil and Cougar mania
When Phil Larder took over, there were two or three good years there [at Keighley]. They got to Old Trafford twice, won once and lost once.

Mick O'Neill and Mike Smith were the main instigators of it. I mean everybody's got their memories of that era, of the early-mid 1990s just before Super League started. One of the funniest ones was, they were playing Batley down at Lawkholme [Lane], Good Friday and it was a horrible night, raining. Jeff Grayshon, I think he was playing for Batley that day. Anyway, Mick O'Neill's on the tannoy system and Batley came out for the start of the game. Keighley were slow coming out

and Mick O'Neill's on the tannoy system going "I can see them – the Cougars. They're getting ready. They're in their cage. They're ready to be let loose. It's feeding time. They're on meat – Batley meat". And everybody's going "hey up". It was brilliant. Oh, it was a really good atmosphere. As I say there was a really good atmosphere because they painted them paws on to the tarmac going into ground. Cougar paw marks that led to changing rooms. It was funny stuff.
Dave Ingham

Maurice Lindsay
In my early days I was banned from Central Park by the then vice-chairman, who became the chairman, and Lord God Protector of rugby league, Maurice Lindsay and we've joked about it since. But Maurice had a particular way of wanting his club reported. When I was working for the agency, they had a player called David Stephenson who wasn't turning up for training and hadn't played for a couple of games. So I was ringing the club up and saying "What's going on?" and wasn't getting anything from them. So what does every good journalist do? He goes to the other side of the story and I rang David Stephenson up direct. This was when they were part-time and he was working as an insurance man in Lytham, I think.

I rang him up at home and said "Look, what's the story?" and he said "Well, basically," and he was a Great Britain international, "I want more money. My contract's coming to an end and I want more money. Wigan aren't wiling to give me more money on a new contract. So I've got an offer from Leeds and I'm thinking about going to Leeds." So I wrote the story. In those days our agency was very well respected and rugby league was probably covered a bit better than it is now.

We had a page lead in every national newspaper, *Mail*, *Express*, *Sun*, *Mirror*, *Telegraph*, the *Today* newspaper as was. They all carried this story and Maurice rang me up, fuming and he's saying "How dare you, how dare you do this story?" I said "Well Maurice, you wouldn't tell me what was happening, so I spoke to David, what's your problem?" He said "You said he's in dispute. He's not in dispute. That's a blurring of the facts!" So I said, "Well what is the truth in it?" He said "Well he wants more money and we're not willing to give it to him". So I said "Well is that not a dispute Maurice?" and he said "Don't be so cheeky, you're banned from Central Park." So that was it, I was banned from Central Park. I put the phone down thinking "What am I going to do?"

Anyway, the next day Maurice rang me and it was as if the conversation had never taken place. He had another story he wanted putting out. That was the thing about Maurice, you could have a stand-up row with him one day and no one mentioned it the day after.
Dave Woods

St John Ellis and Kelvin Skerrett

I ghosted a column for St John Ellis, a fantastic column. I mean ghosted columns are things that I really enjoy doing and his was, I think, the first I did. This was in the *Rugby Leaguer*. Basically, with ghosted columns, they do reflect what the player is like and Singe, I mean he was a flighty player, a will o' the wisp player. He'd come in here and we'd sit and talk for half an hour, "I can't think of anything Phil" and float off.

There was one fantastic occasion. We've got cats and while we were talking one cat came in with a mouse in its mouth and the mouse escaped and went under a settee. Singe lifts the settee up so the cat can get the mouse, and I get the settee to pull it down so the cat can't get the mouse and we're running round my living room with a settee. I'd always imagined somehow, before I did this, that ghosted columns would be at the Ritz or somewhere and you'd have a leisurely meal paid for by the paper. But no, I ghosted a column with Singe and one with Kelvin Skerrett.

Kelvin Skerrett, is a friend of mine, he's our coach at Methley Royals now, and this taught me a lesson. I'd written things about Kelvin on the image of a bruising, thick prop and then I ghosted his column. Brian Smith pulled me one match at Keighley and said "Who's writing this column on Kelvin Skerrett?" I said "I am." He said "He doesn't talk like that." I said "He does." I tidied it up, but Kelvin made very intelligent thoughtful comments.

Phil Hodgson

Dewsbury and Eddie Waring

Dewsbury chairman George Oldroyd welcomes the 26-year-old
Eddie Waring to Crown Flatt. (Courtesy Harry Waring)

A wartime Dewsbury team, probably before the 1941 Yorkshire Cup Final at
Huddersfield, when they lost 15–5 to Bradford Northern. Eight of the players
were 'guests' from other clubs who were stationed near Dewsbury. Jim
Sullivan is fifth from the left in the back row. Eddie Waring is one from the
right in the back row (Courtesy Harry Waring)

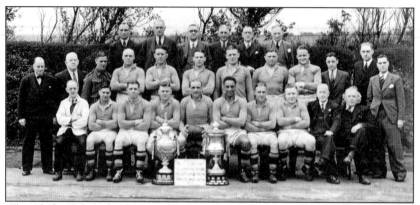

The 1942–43 Dewsbury team that won the Championship, Challenge Cup and Yorkshire Cup, although the Championship was declared null & void because they had fielded an ineligible player. Their team for the Challenge Cup Final included eight 'guests'. (Courtesy Harry Waring)

Dewsbury versus Widnes at Crown Flatt, Championship semi-final in 1947. Dewsbury won 5–2, but lost in the Final to Wigan. (Courtesy Robert Gate)

years on, makes me misty eyed. I remember it also as a good humoured occasion when families and friends travelled to give thanks and pay tribute to the capital after six years of war.

This year will be my 41st Final and although I will miss the Twin Towers I know that the New Wembley Stadium will be even better than its predecessor and the RFL will have no problem in filling it for years to come.

During all the Wembley years from 1946 to 1999 there has never been any crowd trouble at our Cup Final which remains a day out for the family, when elders tell children stories of great players of yesteryear, of memorable matches and deeds of "derring-do". Long may our rugby league values continue.

Harry Waring

The 1946 Indomitables

When we were selected it was all very, very quick – we had to get measured for blazers and everything. We all assembled in London to go on the journey. It was a wonderful experience really. I suppose it was like a schoolboy's dream almost and the party we went with were wonderful people.

The welcome you got in Australia was fantastic. We'd been through the war and they couldn't do enough for you. The journey on the boat was good. We got everything from the Navy, got kitted out with white shorts and white shirts for going through the Mediterranean.

We dined with the Warrant Officers and there was 12 Welshmen [in the party]. Put 12 Welshmen together and they want to sing. Ike Owens was very keen on this idea of a Welsh choir, but they didn't want to split the party up, so everybody was in the Welsh Choir. We'd give concerts every night to the sailors and then when we got to Australia we were invited all over the place. Ike was the conductor, he was the soloist, Martin Ryan was a good singer, it was a bonding thing really. If there'd been a Welsh Choir on its own it would have separated you. But it didn't do that. Ike said let's all be in it and it was a bit [of a] success. In fact Ike was that keen he was putting notices up 'Choir practice at 3 o'clock!'

I have a photograph of us all waiting for the Cornish Express to take us to Southampton and we boarded the Indomitable. It was wonderful, there were miners, shipyard workers, chemical factory workers, Gus was an officer in the Army, Ernest Ward and one or two others were still in service and got permission to leave. We all got together and the friendship really lasted a lifetime, Frank Whitcombe, Trevor Foster, people like that, it was great.

We trained every day on the ship. It was such a good flight deck. It was a big help really. When we got to Freemantle the ship had to come back to England and we were left in an Army camp for a week.

Bev Risman, Joe Egan, Mike Stephenson and Bryn Knowelden at The George Hotel in March 2009 for the reunion of the 1946 Lions tourists.
(Photo: Peter Lush)

Then they said there was a train going from Fremantle to Sydney. It was just an ordinary train and it took five days and five nights. We just slept as we were in our suits and we had meals by the side of the train sat in the sand hills. We got good food and as soon as the train stopped, the Aboriginals came out from all over. They got what was left of the meal. It was rough but you saw Australia, you went past old mines and through little towns in the desert. We called at all the big cites, Perth, Melbourne and Adelaide.

The travelling accommodation was rough [throughout the tour]. You'd be going up to Queensland on a train for 12 or 14 hours. I think having been through the War you'd kind of got used to it, that everything didn't go straight for you. It was never these fast trains, you know, and lads used to get out, have a run and the train would pick you up. Out of it all I never saw any complaints, even though it wasn't as cushy as people might expect. You carried your kit with you – when you got off the train you had a knife, fork and a spoon. You carried that with you all week. Things ordinary people would think were a bit rough. I have a photograph somewhere, I'm getting on the train and Fred Hughes has got a big bag of straw to sleep on. But you accepted it and when you got to Sydney everything was wonderful. Everywhere we went the whole 26 went.
Bryn Knowelden

Winning the 1946 test series
New South Wales, that was a big match because Risman and McCue had said "This is it now, you've got to show them". Of course, we'd a

wonderful pack of forwards: Ken Gee, Joe Egan, Frank Whitcombe, Trevor Foster, Doug Phillips, Ike Owens, and we won about 14–10. The press, they play a big part in Australian rugby league, and the headlines the next morning were "The only way you'll beat this team is to sign Primo Carnera, Jack Dempsey, Joe Louis" and about six world champions. That impression carried everything forward.

I only played in the test match in New Zealand. [In Australia] we drew the first [test match] and Jack Kitching got sent off, that was in Sydney. Then we went right up into Townsville and came down to play in Brisbane and won that quite well. Then the final one in Sydney, we won that quite well. You were always battling for your place, but the competition was very good. I mean when we went it was Gus Risman and Ernest Ward were centres, then Martin Ryan had a rupture, Gus went to full-back and Jack Kitching came in. Then I think Gus went back to centre.

So competition was very good, but it didn't affect anything, everybody stuck together. One of the proudest things for me was, we'd been to Townsville and were coming down for the second test. Gus Risman and McCue were unavailable. It was the only time one of them didn't captain the team. We had our breakfast and it come through on the tannoy, "Would Knowelden go to the managers' room", and I went. "I'm giving you the honour today of being captain" he [Mr Popplewell, the team manager] said, "I like the work you've done." It was quite a proud moment. I have a photograph and I remember sitting on the form surrounded by Trevor Foster, Frank Whitcombe, Doug Phillips and I thought to myself "Not bad for a soccer player!"

In the hotel I shared a bedroom with Dai Jenkins, he was a little toughie. Dai was a good half-back, but he never got in, McCue was that good. It upset some and it may have upset Dai a little bit, but he never showed it. Willie Davies never got in the big matches. But they weren't like me, they were stars. I took it as it came, really, I mean you wanted to be in, but the bonding was wonderful. It didn't matter whether you were in the top matches, you got the same treatment.

Pat Devery was captain [of Australia], Lionel Cooper came to Huddersfield with Pat, Johnny Hunter was the full-back, Arthur Clues came to Leeds, Harry Bath came to Barrow. They were the main ones [players for Australia] and they had a lad from up the country played centre, he came to Leeds, Teddy Verenkamp. So they were quite good, but they'd never met forwards like [ours] before. I mean they came to England to improve themselves, they were raw lads.

The first match against New South Wales, they had a forward called 'Bumper' Farrell, who was the tough guy of Australia. He was up against Ken Gee. He couldn't get away from Ken quick enough. We mastered them in the first match and it was such a big thing. But it had been planned all the way over. New South Wales, they were the top team, with Arthur Clues and Harry Bath and 'Bumper' Farrell. 'Bumper' Farrell was world famous in Australia for being a tough guy, but Ken Gee massacred him. It was rough.

Bryn Knowelden

The Challenge Cup Final replay, Odsal, 1954

Oh, the press got on about the replay at Odsal, and were quoting how many would be there and things. A big match at Odsal in them days, a semi-final, got 60,000 and they talked about another 60,000. They never expected double. It was an unbelievable crowd.

We didn't expect what happened you know. We [the Halifax team] met at Bull Green. We got on the coach. I know somebody said, "Hell, there's a lot of traffic coming down King Cross", which was the Warrington traffic. It came through Halifax and going over North Bridge. We realised just how much traffic there was. The driver said "I'm going to miss this job" and rang the police. Two motorcyclists came and actually they took us on to Hipperholme and we went round that way and came at the bottom side, which we found out was better.

The main road through Northowram was just clogged up. There were a lot of people got that far and no further. The police said we'll take you this other way and we went through every light and everything. We were like royalty. Some of the lads were acting daft, you know. Cars were pulling up and playing hell.

There were a lot stopped and knocked on houses in Northowram and said "Can we listen to the wireless?" They got out of the car because it were stopped on the road and they thought, 'Oh we'll never get there'.

[At the ground] they knocked a gate down, you know, and they just trampled over it. Well nobody could take money off them. It was just a surge of folk come in, and they estimated about 20,000 came in and didn't pay. They always said there was about 120,000.

Well we didn't know what was happening. One or two came in and said "By there's a good crowd!" You know how they talk, like, "looks a good crowd that". Now ten to seven when we came out, there's about 20 yards to walk before you meet the steps. Well, as you come out, there's just a crowd around you and they're all patting you on the back, going down [to the pitch] you see.

We went through the crowd and they're all shouting "Come on Halifax", you know, and then you just got to the top and looking down, it just took your breath away. It were unbelievable. You stopped in your tracks and said "Oh!" Never seen a crowd like that and then we walked down the steps and by the time we got on the field and looked around it was unbelievable. But we soon got going and you forgot about it.

The match wasn't bad. Well they always said it was exciting, because two or three minutes to go we were still thinking we could win it. He just got a late try did Gerry Helme.
Ken Dean

Double heartbreak – watching Halifax in 1956
I remember going to big games and I suppose the biggest one was going up to Odsal when we [Halifax] beat Wigan in 1956, 11–10. We were losing 5–0 and Ken Dean dived over under the posts just before half-time at our end. There were 52,273 there that day, fantastic.

When you think of the crowds they brag about today, if they get 25,000 for a game they think they have done well. But 52,273 at Odsal and it had atmosphere. Then in the second half Wigan went in front and somebody must have thumped Geoff Palmer, because he always played better when somebody thumped him. I can remember we were at the other end, they were at the 'Muck' end, we were at the Rooley Lane end. I can remember him [Palmer] taking about four over near the corner flag and then he scored another and we won. We only kicked one goal, so we had three tries and one goal to their two tries and two goals, when the try was a three point try.

That was a great day because Wigan are the Manchester United of rugby league. Mum wouldn't let me go to Wembley so again I listened to it on the radio. There was a roar and I heard the commentators say what I thought was "Palmer" but it was "Carlton" for St Helens that had scored. The elation and deflation, I thought we'd scored and they'd scored. We lost that 13–2 and I can remember the players coming back from Wembley. They came past the old Ramsden brewery on Huddersfield Road, we were stood there and watched them in an open-top bus.

The following Saturday they went to Maine Road and I managed to go – we lost that game in the last minute. We had scored three tries to their two and it was 9–8, [with a] couple of minutes to go. We got penalised for offside. Colin Hutton, the full-back, kicked the goal and took the Championship out of our hands. That was a real sickener. We climbed over the fence and went onto the field. They were all milling around us singing *Old Faithful* and as a 12 or 13 year old I cried my eyes out, I was really upset.

The crowd that day was 36,675, [but] Maine Road [seemed] packed, there were no restrictions on gates then. It was a ticket game but they opened the turnstiles and as I say it was really upsetting and going home, the faces on the coach going from Maine Road back to Halifax were rather glum. We weren't happy bunnies at all and my mum didn't need to ask how they'd gone on because she could tell when I walked in the door by the look on my face.
Geoff Wright

Beating the Aussies

[I first went to Australia for the World Cup in] 1957. That was really good, but they beat us. Then in 1960 we beat them easy. We should have won all three [world cup tournaments in 1954, 1957 and 1960]. But things happen that can turn a game. We had some hard games, but I've a lot of mates over there so I can't have been that bad!

We had a good side [in 1958]. The Aussies would always shout what they were going to do and all this, I said "Let them talk we'll see". Anyway we beat them. It was one each and we beat them in the final [test]. We lost the first one to get the gate up! They don't like it when you say that.

But that 1962 team was good team, we should have won the lot. They got a penalty and kicked it in the last minute. I got sent off in that match, I was unlucky, [the referee was] Darcy Lawler[17]. I came off and all the nutters in the crowd were shouting and bawling and throwing stuff. So I picked an apple up and said "Throw some more!" and they all cheered us after that. Ashton said "You lost us that" I said "If I hadn't have tackled that centre, he'd have scored under the sticks anyway so it wouldn't have made any difference, because you lot wouldn't have tackled him." He said "Yeah, but I've told you, Mick, about that" [the high tackle]. I said "I don't usually get pulled up, it was Lawler anyway he gave them it. We've won the Ashes". He said "Yeah, but we'd have been the first since so and so [to win all three tests]". I said "You didn't get any more [money], did you!"

[In 1958] we'd lost the first and we played at Brisbane. It was a hard game. But you've got to play the referee, it's no good moaning when you go to Australia, you know you're not going to get owt. Anyway we were in front, they took the lead and we got it back and finished up winning. But we'd about three or four injured. Preckie played all the match with his shoulder (dislocated)[18]. We beat them anyway in the decider in Sydney, like. We butchered them, I scored three. That's the last time anyone's scored three against the Aussies. It might be a long time too the way they're going. But they keep moaning all the time. It's no good moaning, knock them down.

They were always saying what they'd do and I used to love it that. I thought well he's got to get past me if he's going to score. It doesn't matter how you win, you don't get two chances. We had some great times and I got on well with all the Aussies. Me and Murph once went out and I didn't drink then. This bloke says "Are you coming up to the club for a drink?" and we went up. We were talking to these Aussies and he said "Who do you think is the best scrum half?" to Murph. He said "You're speaking to him!" and he was

---

[17] An Australian referee who had a reputation for favouring Australia.

[18] In fact Alan Prescott broke his arm early in the match.

only, like 18! They said "That Diamond will kill you". I said "He'll have to run without his head," there was uproar! But he (Murphy) definitely believed what he said.

Mick Sullivan

Heartache and ecstasy – two weeks in 1962

In 1962 we went to both finals, Wembley and the Championship. We got beat at Wembley by Wakefield and the following week we're playing in the Championship final at Bradford and if they'd have beat us they'd have won all four cups. But we beat them.

Just before the end of the game I scored the try that sealed it and I've never seen as many people on a rugby field. Not because I'd scored, but because of the electricity. Wakefield were a very, very good side. On paper they had a better side than us. But we had good morale. We'd some lads with some really exceptional skills, but we were a unit more than being brilliant and it was up for grabs. They only just beat us at Wembley. Neil Fox won the Lance Todd Trophy, he dropped three goals. They called it the 'drop-goal final'. He scored a try as well.

You know people talk about nerves before a game and I think everybody gets a bit that way before games. But when you go to a game like that, it's something different. Wembley was different. It's hard to explain really and it's hard to believe that anybody could say they didn't have any nerves.

What I did find – as daft as it sounds – that when I'd been out there 10 minutes, I wouldn't say it was just another game, but you'd a greater will to win than any before. I mean you want to win any game you play, don't you? You can't enjoy a game unless you're playing well. But it was different. It was the biggest crowd I'd played in front of.

I think it [losing at Wembley] made us more determined to win the next week. Like I say on paper they were quite a bit better than us, but our lads would get stuck in. Every week they were the same and we had good morale, it was brilliant in the dressing room.

Tommy Smales

The battle of Headingley, 1963

I've seen a lot of test matches over the years and there are certain ones that stick out like the 1963 third test at Headingley.

[Australia had] beaten Britain down at Wembley. Then they went to the second test at Swinton, which I went to, and inflicted the biggest defeat on Britain in their history up to that point.

People like Alex Murphy, Vince Karalius were playing and Neil Fox. They sustained a load of injuries that particular day, Great Britain, and picked a completely different side to play the third test at Headingley, which was just an absolute battle from start to finish.

I can remember I were in the paddock at Leeds, which was the area just under the main stand. I'm just one side of the halfway line and Aussies kicking off. And everybody expected it was going to be a rough, tough match and it certainly was. I mean it's gone down as 'the battle of Headingley'. Three got sent off.

Kenny Roberts was [in the pack] that day. He stood on the touchline for the kick off on the 10-yard line. The Aussies were kicking off and I can remember people in crowd shouting "Go on Kenny, give them it". He just turned round and winked and he had his fists clenched and that was the start of things to come, because when the Aussies come charging through he just went in, they went in battering them.

I think the first scrum down, all the front-row were up and at each other. They won that game, but, as I say, three got walked, a game you'll never ever forget. Not particularly for the rugby league, but for, I wouldn't say 'thuggery', but battles that were going on, on the field. Well, it was rugby league in the raw was that.
Dave Ingham

Winning at Wembley with Featherstone, 1967

We [Featherstone Rovers] had a meeting at a pub Alan Hardisty took over in Castleford. I'd just got a packet of 20 Embassies and the [Challenge Cup] draw came on. I says "There, I've finished smoking until we get knocked out" and we drew Bradford who were top of the table. So the bloke I'd given six cigarettes to said "You'll not be stopping smoking long, will you?" I never had a cig then while I came off the field at Wembley and the first thing I did was go to a supporter for a cig. It was when we went up for the cup, I cadged a cig.

We were at [home to] Wakefield in the second round and they were top of the table, I think they were all top of the table when we played them. Then Castleford and Leeds, in the semi-final at Fartown. [The key was] team spirit, we all worked for one another. Laurie Gant, he was a big influence on us. His team talks were brilliant.

We went down [to London] on Wednesday. Trained at Crystal Palace. We stayed at Crystal Palace. On the Saturday we went to Wembley in the morning and went on the field. I remember Tommy Smales, he got a ball and had his boots on. He put the ball down on the pitch and stood back to take a kick at goal. One of the stewards came up "You can't do that", "How do you mean?" "You're not allowed to do it," "I'm doing it". "You can't!" He stood in front of the ball and I think it was Arnie Morgan grabbed hold of him and pulled him back. Tommy had a go at goal and kicked it.

Going down Wembley way was brilliant. I mean Featherstone, it's only a small place. It not like St Helens, Wigan and Leeds. There were very little nerves in the dressing room, it was surprising. I was 26 then and [one of] the oldest in the side. Brian Wrigglesworth was the oldest. But the others were maybe a year younger than me or something like that. So they weren't experienced as real experience goes.

[Walking out] was out of this world. You hear the chanting and when you got to the tunnel entrance it just erupted, you know, and then all the way down to the centre, they just went mad. It's a smashing feeling and what made it better was the Queen presented the cup. So that made it something to remember. [Prince] Phillip came round and was introduced to the teams. I was surprised, because he was only a little bloke and I thought he was a big bloke.

But after we'd numerous do's and people used to say "What did the Queen say to you?" I couldn't remember. So I had to make summat up, like, "Is your wife here?" and I said "Yes she's sat at the back, in fact she's got the same colour suit on as you." "Oh, very good". She didn't say that, but I'd make it up to get them off my back, they wouldn't let it rest.

[It was] brilliant, you couldn't believe it. Tears, tears of happiness, hugs, you know, it was brilliant. It's something you don't think of a little town team doing. One player was from Rossington, Mick Smith, stand-off half, he lived in Rossington at Doncaster. But Brian Wrigglesworth lived in Castleford, Vaughan Thomas lived at Sharlston, Keith Cotton lived at Castleford, Gary Jordan lived in Pontefract, Kenny Greatorex lived in Featherstone, Dooler lived at Sharlston, Tonky lived at Featherstone, Graham Harris lived at Normanton, I lived at Pontefract then, and Jimmy Thompson, Arnie Morgan and Tommy Smales lived in Featherstone.
Malcolm Dixon

"He wasn't allowed to forget" – Don Fox and Wembley 1968
In 1968, the Watersplash Final when he (Don Fox) missed the kick. David Coleman came as he was walking down the tunnel and says "Commiserations Don, I know you've missed the kick and I know you've lost, but I'd like to congratulate you, you've won the Lance Todd Trophy". Don says, quote, "Stick it up thi arse" to David Coleman. He said "I don't want it." So, later on when they'd calmed him down, they had to go through it all again and if you see it, he's tears in his eyes and he's saying "Thank you, I'm sorry everybody" and he was heartbroken.

I was with him, because I knocked about with him in them days, with my brother Gordon and my brother Barry. We were in a wine bar somewhere in London, I don't know where, and the press were all over, cameras were all over and everybody wanted Don Fox. He was having a drink, going outside, getting interviewed and going back in. There were cameras inside and they just wouldn't leave him alone. It was like paparazzi. Anyway, they came to him and they said "Don, we want you to go on the London Palladium, Sunday night." He said "No chance, I'm going back to the fans."

He went on that balcony and waved to the fans and he was absolutely fantastic. It's got some effect on me, so it must have had some effect on him. There were placards: "We love Don Fox, We love Don Fox", thousands of them, this was in Wakefield. The reception he got was out of this world. So he would never have forgotten that. When you used to talk to him he'd say "Of all the goals I kicked, the only one they remember me for is the one I missed". That's the thing that did hurt him. They showed it year after year after year and he wasn't allowed to forget it.

Graham Chalkley

Tragedy and triumph – the 1969 Championship Final
Roy Francis had just been sacked by Hull. Not a lot of people know this, they think Roy left Hull to come to Leeds. But Roy had been given the order of the boot by Hull and was looking for something to do. As he said to me: "I've always found in my career when one door closes another one opens and this other one opening was at Leeds."

So he came across to see me and Noel [Stockdale]. I knew Roy from his Wigan days. He used to go dancing at the Empress Ballroom in Wigan and I knew what type of person he was. A lot of charisma, he could get players eating out of his hand. He was appointed then and stayed with us until we won the Cup at Wembley.

Anyway, he said to me when we won the Cup, "Right Joe, I'm off, I'm going to North Sydney. They've been in touch with me and we've been in correspondence for some time. They want me to go to Australia and I want to try the Australian scene. We've won the Cup at Wembley there's only way for the club now and that's down, so I'm off."

So off he went to North Sydney, where he had a pretty unsuccessful run I'm afraid. We appointed, temporarily, Jack Nelson, a local lad who had come to help me with the juniors. [He] had been a great help, great lad and he was nominated to a post he never aspired to. Coach at Leeds was beyond his wildest dreams. Anyway, I gave him all the help I could and we got on very well. He took over and at Christmas that year Castleford were top, we were second and we were playing Castleford on Boxing Day.

Christmas Day, the phone rang and it was Jack's wife "Can you come over? Jack's died." I was shattered. Anyway, I went across. They were just taking Jack's body out of the house and his family were distraught. I stayed with them doing what I could. I rang the chairman to let him know and he came over to the house and helped and the question was "What's going to happen the next day?" The lads were going to come and find the man they trained with the previous night wasn't there any more.

So Jack [Myerscough, the Leeds director of football] asked me would I take over – and I did. It was very traumatic. The lads were coming up to the dressing room full of bounce and Christmas bonhomie and all for this big match against Castleford, beat them and we go top and I'm having to say "I've got some very bad news. Jack's died." Well they were shattered.

So I arranged to take them up to the ballroom in the pavilion, which was empty before the match in those days. I had an array of skipping ropes and medicine balls, anything to keep their minds off this tragedy. Then we went out and we won, we beat Cas. And of course everybody's happy about that and we go top of the league and stayed top of the league for the rest of the season.

I carried on coaching for the rest of that year and we arranged to bring in Derek Turner, whose praises I was singing as a leader of men. I'd have been happy to carry on. But they'd made up their minds early on that Derek would be joining us and weren't going to go back on it, which I was perfectly happy about. It just meant that I was the first successful Championship-winning coach to be replaced by the coach of the side he'd just beaten!

[The final] was decried as being a blood-and-guts game, bad for the game and in fact I had to write a letter of defence in to the *Yorkshire Post*. I wrote to Alf Drury[19] and he said his editor had seen the letter and he'd like to use it as an article, did I mind? I didn't and it was published. I was defensive of our players and the game in general. Young [Barry] Seabourne had dislocated his shoulder earlier on in that season and in several games it had come out. At Odsal it came out two or three times and he came to sideline and had it pushed back. His face was white and he was obviously in agony. So at half-time I had to bring him off.

Then there were a couple of sendings off. Mal Reilly was sent off I remember. It was a blood-and-guts game and at half-time my feelings were "If you can keep your heads when all around are losing theirs" sort of thing and in the end the cool head of Risman won the day because he fielded a ball, made a bit of progress with it and kicked for John Atkinson. Atky scored and that was it. I mean Atky didn't get a tremendous lot of credit for it, but taking the ball no matter how kind the bounce is at full speed and the game hinging on it. I pay my tribute to John Atky for that try [and] for all the hundreds of others he scored.

Joe Warham

---

[19] The *Yorkshire Post's* rugby league correspondent.

Geoff Gunney and Alf Burnell before the 1954 Lions tour.
(Courtesy *Rugby League Journal*)

Karl Harrison in action for Great Britain against Australia in 1990.
(Courtesy *Rugby League Journal*)

The 1929 Challenge Cup Final: Wigan 13 Dewsbury 2. (Courtesy Peter Lush)

The 1934 Challenge Cup Final: Hunslet 11 Widnes 5. (Courtesy Harry Waring)

A brave decision – the 1971 Challenge Cup Final

Well it was a rough, tough game, I sent one off in 1971. I sent Syd Hynes off, the Leeds centre, on a touch judge's intervention. He said he viciously butted him [Alex Murphy] in the face and I sent him off.

I always had that with my touch judge, we had a perfect understanding. You have got to get it right, it's a team that goes out. The orders are "All the help that you can give me" and "What's on the ball is mine, what's off the ball is yours." [When] I see a bloke laid down 20 or 30 [yards] away from play I want to know what happened. When he comes to tell me I want to know, in your opinion does he go off or does he stay on, you've seen it and at Wembley Terry Clayton from Widnes, I hold my hands up to him, he was a brave man. He said "viscously butted him" and in his opinion he should be dismissed. I sent him off and now there was uproar. [They were] saying "Murphy was winking on the stretcher" and "he conned you Thompson". He conned the St John's Ambulance Brigade and all because they put him on the stretcher and took him off. It says in a book of great finals he came back to play a part. He never came back at all, he only came back to receive the cup. He never came back on and it says in the book, these that know it all, said that he played the game out. He never came back, he came back to collect the cup and I believe Derek Turner, the Leeds coach, had a go at him, but nowt to do with me is it.

You ask anybody connected with Leeds, they've had Alex Murphy speaking at their dinners and Syd Hynes has been there and you can still never get anything out of him. You cannot get anything. Murphy won't say anything, Sid Hynes won't say anything.

All I can tell you is this, that the incident happened on the Royal Box side and when I sent Sid Hynes he was the down the other side of the pitch, I'll leave it with you. I'll accept responsibility. Nobody has mentioned Terry Clayton, it's always been me. But I'll give the man the guts for having to do it. I can hold my hand up and very rarely can I say a bloke that ran the line for me was a dummy. I never had one. I didn't have them. Everybody can make a mistake, but blatantly missing, looking the other way when somebody's got one, that ain't it.

But I'd say to anybody "If you wanna have a go, you have a go at refereeing." It's a tough thing to do. It's tough. The teams want to win, the chairman of each team wants his team to win, the supporters want their team to win, the tea ladies are die-hards and they want their team to win. So where's your support? It's nil isn't it? So you accept it and have a smile on your face and wave to them.
Billy Thompson

The battle of Lang Park – Wales versus England
1975 World Cup

We drew with the Aussies and New Zealand, we beat France home and away, we beat Wales over here. In those days[20] it was a points system and we beat the Aussies over here, we beat the Kiwis over here. But the Battle of Lang Park, England and Wales, they kicked seven bells out us and that cost us the World Cup. It ended up with us on 12 points [in the final table] and the Aussies on 13.

I played number nine that game, Bridgie got injured at Gimpy against Toowoomba. We played on the Wednesday against Wales at Lang Park. [The Welsh pack was] Mills, Fisher, Wanbon, Eddie Cunningham, Dixon, Coslett, Mantle on the bench and there was blokes like Watkins, Bill Francis and Maurice Richards [in the backs]. They were a good team.

We stopped in the best hotel in Brisbane, with a terrace and things, we had taxis to take us to training, we had all the best gear and it rankled with the Welsh. Les Pearce was the coach of Wales and they used to have to run to training and we'd be waiting outside our hotel for the taxis and [Alex] Murphy [the England coach] would be "Pearce, you couldn't coach greyhounds".

It got to [a stage where], if you saw Bill Francis – my big mate Bill from Featherstone who played in the same team as Eric Chisnall – he'd walk on the other side of the road. So you knew it was going to kick off. The Aussies were sat in the stand watching, they must have been laughing their bloody caps off.

I remember the first scrum down, Chissy was at eight and Mike Coulman at ten. Mills, Fisher and Wanbon, they did everything. The next scrum, he got Chissy [Eric Chisnall] and nutted him, did Millsy and it just kicked off. A fella called Lancaster was refereeing and you know how sometimes they get in and stop it, well he was 'just leave them to it!' You've never seen owt like it, there were fists and boots flying and everything. He got both captains together, Roger [Millward] and David Watkins, I sidled up, I thought "I've a bit of a vested interest here" and he ordered a scrum down again, I thought "I can't believe it!"

It cost us the World Cup, we lost 12–7. Wales then played the Aussies on the Saturday and the Aussies towelled them, we played them [Australia] the week after and we drew 10 apiece. They still talk about that in Australia, 'the battle of Lang Park'.

Mick Morgan

---

[20] The 1975 World Cup was decided on a league system played over one year.

A clash of cultures – BARLA's 1978 southern hemisphere tour

The second game we played at Lae and that was a pretty bad area apparently, but we didn't know. It was a night match. When the coach took us into the back of the stadium I noticed all these vehicles, pick up trucks with a wire cage on the back, about 20 of them lined up. I thought it must have been a construction company or something. As the game progressed, they were fenced in the ground, the spectators, about 6,000 there,

all Papua New Guinea people. They were getting really excited. With about eight minutes to go they were winning 4–2 and just came over the barriers. The fence was about 10 foot high, they all climbed over it. It was absolutely unbelievable, "what's going on here like?"

There were literally hundreds and hundreds of lads on the field knocking the hell out of the English players. They came over the stands where we were and you finished up defending yourself.

All of a sudden we heard the rifle shots and everybody dispersed and then we found out what the pick-up trucks with cages were for. They were just firing them into the back of them, locking them in and then wheeling them off. We finished up in the changing rooms and they laid siege to the changing rooms for about three hours, they were really hostile.

I also remember this Papua New Guinea lad coming in, a police inspector, but had been to Oxford University. Looked to be about middle 30s, very smart with his police uniform on, threequarter socks, shorts and he had a swagger stick, his cap was like a guards cap, cut down. He had these massive lobes, with a hole in. About three eighths of an inch across, they were long because they put weights on the opening of the ear and the longer the lobes, the higher prestige they have. He said "you've been fortunate tonight, really fortunate". I said "Bit naughty is this". One of the lads got that badly hurt he never played again on tour. They got kicked up and down the field, not a nice experience.

Our next game was up in the mountain district, up in Mount Hagan. He said "If you think you've had it bad here, wait until you get up into the mountain district, they'll murder you". They insisted on more security up there. We went up there, and what was happening, we found out, we were playing the game too physical. They weren't used to that physical side of it. Being a hot country

were 10,000 or not, but it really came alight in the second test which they took to Melbourne, down at the Park Stadium.

They'd lost the first test at the Sydney Football Ground. One guy saved Australia that day and that was Andrew Ettingshausen, who'd been at Leeds as a player just prior to that series. Had he not played full-back that day I think we would have been home and dry because he caught Martin Offiah twice, which if you'd been a betting man you wouldn't have put your money on anybody catching Offiah. But he copped him twice when you thought Offiah was clear, or 'Offyer' as the Aussies say.

Then the second test in Melbourne was when hordes of the supporters came over and really made their presence felt. That was when they dished out the heaviest defeat the Australians suffered at the hands of Britain on their own soil. Brilliant, I mean unbelievable. I'd come down from Brisbane. We were stopping up in Brisbane because my wife's auntie lives up there and we'd gone from Sydney after the first test up to Cairns and come back down to her house to stay with her. There was no way I was going to miss this match, so I flew down from Brisbane and met up with some people from Keighley who stopped in the same hotel. They drank the hotel completely dry that night.

We actually featured on *Look North* because when we were walking down to the stadium prior to the match [TV presenter] Harry Gration were there with the TV cameras, just walking round. He stopped us and said "Can you go back and come down and look as though you're going to cheer them on?"

There was a band started. Roy Dickinson from Leeds had a tour party, and they were with some lads from Silsden. They'd all linked up and got white bowler hats and a drum and you could hear this 'boom', 'boom', 'boom', 'boom'. Then this band – there would be probably about 20 of them at the time – just absolutely grew in numbers between the second and third test which was at Lang Park.

When we went up to Lang Park they'd acquired more musical instruments and more members of the band with white bowler hats on. They came over this hill and straight across the dual carriageway without even looking, stopped the traffic and everything. Half of them had no tickets, but they just opened the gates and let them in, and then the Aussies were hurling tinnies at them, you know, from out the ground.

But yes, brilliant experience going on tour. I mean they really made you welcome, in spite of the fact that they reckon they hate the Poms. They don't.

Dave Ingham

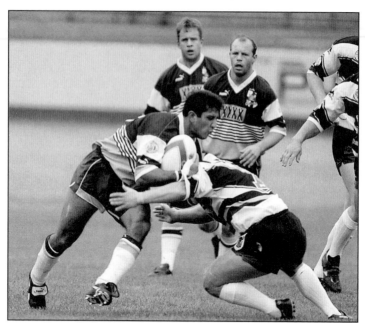
Ikram Butt taking the ball up for the London Broncos.
(Courtesy Ikram Butt)

The symbol of Cougarmania at Keighley.
(Photo: Peter Lush)

7.   Super League and the modern era

Doing what had to be done

We formed the Parliamentary Rugby League Group and there was a lot of political activity around discrimination against rugby league by rugby union. One of my colleagues at the time, Roger Stott, had attempted to press the issue of 'Sport for All'. The Sport England – or whatever it was – symbol and charter apparently made it illegal for union to do what it had been doing for donkey's years. So we started a campaign very early on to try and highlight the way union discriminated against league and as a consequence affected its development, because kids couldn't play league, and you couldn't play it in the armed forces until we got that changed.

People say union's a global game. Well look at why it's a global game. It's because the British armed forces spread it here, there and everywhere. The same armed forces banned rugby league until 1993 when we got it changed and credit to Iain Sproat the Sports Minister at the time. But we started big style with a campaign in Parliament – a cross party campaign – to the put the boot into union discrimination and the first thing that we did was to try and amend the National Lottery Bill so they realised we were serious.

I moved an amendment to block any grants form the National Lottery to sports or organisations that discriminated and made a speech about union. This got on board one or two people. Ian Sproat, who was a Tory, a rugby union man, knew nothing about all this. Suddenly he realised there was an issue that needed to be sorted out. Amazingly, [our bill] got a second reading into committee. We'd no intention of it actually going into legislation, what we wanted to do was make a point. But the Rugby Football Union took on advisors, they were lobbying against it and in the end, by 1994 they realised the game was up. There was pressure on them from Australia and New Zealand to go pro and we were getting income tax people telling us that the clubs were fiddling their crowds in rugby union and it got pretty heated.

I loved every minute of it and so did my friend Ian McCartney, the MP for Makerfield and many others. I look back with great pride at what we tried to do because it needed doing. Now you look back and you talk to kids of 20, they've no idea that you were banned from playing rugby union for life. I say "I was banned from playing rugby union for life" and they say "What for, gouging, stamping, blinding?" and I say "No, for playing rugby league, not as a professional, as an amateur!"

I got letters from all over the place when I was doing this sports discrimination bill. One I remember vividly was from a prison officer who had worked at a prison where they had a joint prisoner and prison officer rugby union team, somewhere in the Midlands. He ended

League at Parliament: Cliff Spracklen (wearing a Bramley shirt) and Ray Gent present David Hinchliffe MP and Lord Lofthouse with a petition about coverage of rugby league in the media in March 2002. (Photo: Peter Lush)

up being banned because they found out he'd played rugby league. So he couldn't play for this prison team even though, as he put it, there was a murderer in the side. The bloke had committed murder, but because he hadn't played rugby league he was all right to play rugby union. But this bloke who'd played rugby league was banned! Absolutely crazy.

On the Tory side we pulled in quite a lot of interesting people. We had a meeting with Dudley Wood from the RFU, it was a fascinating meeting. I was really worried because we packed this room and there were mainly Tories there. But the right wing Tories were getting stuck into the Rugby Union over discrimination. It was an unbelievable situation! Completely contradictory to what you'd expect.

Michael Joplin who was then an MP – he's now in the House of Lords – told this story about standing as a Tory candidate in Wakefield and I remembered it. It was the first general election that I can really remember, 1959. He was a Tory candidate up against my predecessor but one, Arthur Creech-Jones, and it was traditional in those days for the candidates in a general election to kick off a match at Belle Vue. I think it was Wakefield versus Hunslet. I was at the game. Arthur Creech-Jones kicked off the first half, Joplin kicked off the second half. At this meeting he told us that the following week he got a phone call saying he was banned from his local rugby union club because he'd professionalised himself by doing that. It was absolutely incredible. Speeches like that just swung the meeting. There were guys there who were totally supportive of the apartheid regime in South Africa getting stuck into rugby union.
David Hinchliffe

'Rugby league's going to be a summer game and Wakefield Trinity, Featherstone Rovers and Castleford are going to be merged!'

I remember vividly getting a phone call from a woman at the BBC one Saturday afternoon telling me rugby league was going to be a summer game and Wakefield Trinity, Featherstone Rovers and Castleford are going to be merged. I said "You're joking, come on!" In the end she had to fax me through this sheet to show she wasn't winding me up. So we got some bright spark – and I know who that was – suggesting Wakefield, Featherstone and Castleford would be called Calder, Warrington and Widnes were going to merge and Bradford and Halifax.

We had a debate in Parliament and there's a story behind that. I never applied for a debate. I came home on Friday from Parliament the week this had happened and there was hell on. There were people marching the streets, it was mayhem. I had a phone call from Geoffrey Lofthouse – now Lord Lofthouse – who was then deputy speaker, MP for Pontefract and Castleford. He's been a Featherstone supporter all his life and was as opposed to us merging as I was. Geoff rang up and said "David you've got a debate on this Super League proposal next Wednesday." I said "Geoff I haven't applied for a debate". "You have now", he said. They were queuing up to speak and it got huge coverage. I think what we kicked into touch was the merger issue and we got more money because the Murdoch lot[21] came up with more money for clubs to avoid mergers. It was a very, very difficult issue at the time because undoubtedly the game needed to restructure.

But the idea of merging Castleford and Wakefield and Featherstone denies the reality of the nature of rugby league which is a local community sport. Its strength is about local communities, for goodness sake. So when Wakefield played Cas a couple of years later in a relegation tussle, Belle Vue was packed to the rafters. There were people sitting on roofs trying to watch the game, it was nationally televised. I came from the north of Scotland because they moved the game forward and I was on holiday. Who on earth thought that [the mergers] up? Well I've a good idea who it was. They don't really understand rugby league without any doubt.

The kind of thinking for the future was modelled on soccer. You know: big city games. That's not what it's about. I think you've got to understand that so many of the problems that soccer has are because they've lost that kind of local identity shaped by the community in relation to the club. I think that's something that rugby league has retained and is a great, great strength for the future.

David Hinchliffe

---

[21] Rupert Murdoch who was backing the Super League through News International

'Gerry Wright on Radio Four talking about rugby league'

I was against Richardson[22] wanting to merge and what was rather sad for me was that I was in a minority with David Hinchcliffe and poor old Richard Clarkson who's no longer with us. We fought a rearguard action against the merger. But if it had been left to the bulk of Wakefield Trinity shareholders, we [would have] lost the vote to merge with Castleford and Featherstone, which upset me enormously. By that time Wakefield had been starved of success for so long, I think a lot of people at the margin thought this might be one way of getting into Super League and actually having a bit of success. I think one or two were prepared to sell their birthright on that.

This was before Super League started. I was on a programme called *Shouting the odds* which discussed the mergers and the Super League concept. Ian Clayton was on the same programme. This would be [around] 1995. I joined a group called Rugby League Fans United and we had a slogan 'Ditch the Dish!' The driving forces were Featherstone supporters and one lad from Cas'. I forget the lad from Cas's name, but there was me, Paul Holmes, who was a Featherstone fan, and Glyn Robinson. Actually that's a story in itself, Glyn, who'd played representative under-19s rugby, he's a Wakefield lad really and became chairman of Featherstone Rovers. He's a former mental health nurse, I knew him when I played with a dance band at Stanley Royd Hospital and he was on the nursing staff there. I got to know him through local politics as well.

Anyway we set up this group. I attended about three or four meetings and we produced three brochures. The idea was to more-or-less proselytise the anti-merger thing. But because Murdoch was inextricably linked to the concept of Super League, which was linked to the mergers, it became a bit of an anti-Super League thing as well.

So I was anti-merger and anti-Super League. Then, of course, it got derailed because Cas and Featherstone fans had declared their intentions vehemently and also Jack Fulton and would it be David Poulter and the Cas committee took a view that they could manage without any outside interference. They got in [Super League] because their league placing allowed them to get in. Whereas Wakefield and Featherstone weren't in the relegation berths. But we were 12th, I think, and Featherstone might have been a place above us or a place below us and they allowed London to come up and brought Paris St Germain in.

To emphasis the point I think the most embarrassing time I've had watching Wakefield Trinity was the penultimate match of that season before Super League. Wakefield v Cas at Wheldon Road and they beat Wakefield Trinity 86–0. I managed to stick it out, I just thought 'I don't know what's going to happen to the club'. I think they put a marker

---

[22] Ted Richardson of Wakefield Trinity

down: 'we don't need any Wakefield players, we've just beaten them 86–0.'

Once the mergers had been dropped I stopped going to the Rugby League Fans United meetings, but I think for a time that organisation carried on. The steam was taken out of it because obviously the idea was to preserve the clubs' identities. It was quite a hot potato at the time. I mean Radio 4 actually covered it. I was quoted. There was a bloke on his holidays, and an extract from a meeting I'd had the night before with some people in Wakefield Trinity concert lounge, what's called the Wildcats bar now, was broadcast. He said "Bloody hell, I don't believe it, there's Gerry Wright on Radio 4 talking about rugby league." He was up in some remote part of Scotland and there's my voice booming out against the mergers.

I would argue with Lindsay's point that without the Murdoch money there wouldn't have been a game. I'm a bit more Harry Edgar than Maurice Lindsay, I read Harry Edgar's publications avidly.[23]

If you look back at the 1992 and 1995 World Cup Finals you'll see huge gates for those two matches. You see you can rewrite history, like Stalin did and blot out what went before to suit you or you can use evidence judiciously or figures to emphasise your point of view. It's what's left out that's as important as what's included.

I'm not totally sold on the idea that rugby league was going bust... I speak to a lot of Wiganers and they bemoan the passing of Central Park and up to this last couple of years they've voted with their feet by not going to the JJB. Wigan's gates are on the up again, you can't just keep a culture down.

Similarly Widnes, who felt slighted that they were not given a franchise, were unfortunate. They had a great side in the 1980s and it's not just Wakefield Trinity that spent all their money on players and bonuses. That's the culture of rugby league.

I would say the Sky coverage is very good in terms of presentation. I'm not a big Murdoch fan, but I would agree they do treat the sport credibly. What worries me is that although we've gone on satellite TV, we're not on terrestrial enough. The national newspapers: when I grew up there was a Manchester edition of the *Daily Mirror*, *Daily Mail*, *News Chronicle*, *Daily Herald* and all that. There was far more in the newspapers. I know we're in an internet age, it's not reflected in my house, but most kids will get their information electronically from now on. But if you're a bloke who buys a newspaper and not the trade press and says 'I wonder how Dewsbury have gone on?' You won't even get a result [in some papers]. So in some cases we've gone back.

The product on the field, that's how they describe it now rather than a game, despite losing to Australia you've got to respect the

---

[23] Harry Edgar's *Rugby League Journal* takes a traditional view of the game and has opposed many recent developments.

players. I always think, whatever the administration the players do the clubs proud. It's such a hard game, probably harder now even with interchanges, although we could talk all afternoon about that. But the players, I think, always rescue the game. The spectacle on the field and the players, no problem with that at all, I think it's a marvellous game. Sadly it doesn't get the publicity it deserves, it's still patronised, and we're still in a ghetto. Expansion, great, nobody wants rugby league to be in a closed ghetto all its life.

But if you're talking in business terms, don't neglect your core business for diversification. You look at all kinds of business decision where the core business has been neglected. Rugby league ought to be able to learn from that sort of thing and fly a kite in places like Ireland, Scotland and Wales as long as its back door is secure. There have been societal changes where kids no longer feel the only outlet for their ambitions is the local rugby club. I think you've still got to allow kids in Batley and Dewsbury to actually play semi-pro and we've just got to be a bit careful.

The trouble with rugby league is it could become very polarised between the old traditionalists who don't see any good from what's going on now and the modern-day people who don't see any good with what went before and somewhere along the line there's the truth. Getting that balance right is difficult.

Gerry Wright

'Absolutely fantastic' from the beginning

I have to say from the beginning, Super League was just absolutely fantastic. It went from what was a bit of a drab, 4,000 crowd, winter sport, to be a summer sport, and in those days Super League didn't actually start the season until April. So it really was a summer sport, unlike now when we start the season in February and it's not quite as summery as one might hope.

But they were fabulous times, going to Old Trafford and [Bradford Bulls] beating Wigan to win the Grand Final. I was with my wife and we daren't move at half-time. It was like if we moved then the spell would be broken. It wouldn't all be real.

The first visit to Wembley in the Challenge Cup in 1996, that was great as well, because it wasn't something we expected. We were a new team with an awful lot of new players and a new coach and we played Leeds in the semi-final, who have generally been a good team. I hate to say it, but they have really. I think we went more in hope than in expectation and to win that game was a bit unbelievable really.

We got to Wembley to play St Helens. It was a beautiful day and Saints as usual played their flamboyant rugby. But for a time we were actually winning and again that was another magical moment, "hang on we're going to win this". Unfortunately things went wrong. Three bombs in the air, three drops by the full-back, who perhaps wasn't

wholly at fault. He wasn't really helped by his other players. But during the game Robbie Paul had scored the first hat-trick at Wembley with a magical side-stepping move where he went half the length of the field and scored under the posts. We came out of the ground and we were still elated even though we'd lost. In a way it didn't seem to matter. It did matter because obviously we'd have liked to have won, but we'd got there and hadn't expected to. So that was a great moment as well.
John Downes

Getting into Super League
In 1997 it was whoever got top was promoted, but in 1998 it was the first season that the grand final was played in Super League or the First Division. We won the First Division grand final to gain promotion. We [Wakefield Trinity] beat Featherstone at the McAlpine. It is probably my most memorable game because it meant so much, going from part-time to full-time and you could go and live your dream as a full-time sportsman.

It was massive. We were the strongest side that year, we played very well from early on and two signings made us do that. Garen Casey who was a stand-off from Penrith, a goalkicker, he got us in the right direction and Matt Fuller who played for the club back in the old First Division in 1994. He came back and helped us as well, as a loose-forward with a bit of leadership and experience alongside the kicker Roger Kenworthy who came from Canberra.

Those three players helped the other players around them, some good local players such as myself who wanted to do well for Wakefield and that's what gave us the impetus to go and win. Having those people around you on grand final day was massive. There's a picture of me walking out at the McAlpine. I always know when I'm under a bit of pressure or anxiety, my lips get quite tight, you can see the tension in my face. In this picture you can't see my mouth it's that tightly closed ready for the game.

We went out and got the 12–0 lead, Featherstone came back and I think they went into the lead. Then there was a controversial decision from a touch judge who spotted a knock-on that the referee had missed, and rightly so. Featherstone would have scored but they got pulled back and I managed to score the final try seven minutes from time and we went 24–22 up.

It was a nailbiter, but I'm glad we came through in the end. Games like that when it's so tight and you put so much in are enormous at the end, because you've given everything. Commiserations to the Featherstone team because they'd have given everything as well. So as much as we were elated they felt the opposite end of the spectrum.

We came back here [Belle Vue] to rapturous applause from the fans. We all had club suits then which we don't have now and ties round our heads. We stayed here for many a night, somebody lost the cup and it ended up in the kit man's boot room so he put it safely away. But I think there were a couple of hours where there was a panic on. It's funny: the First Division grand final cup is a silver ball with a kangaroo on one side and a Welsh dragon on the other. I'd be interested to find out the historical significance of that cup because obviously it was never designed to be a First Division trophy, it has been recycled from an Aussie-Welsh competition.

As a club and as a playing team there was a lot to do. It's a big prospect playing in Super League and everyone anticipated we wouldn't get in to start with. I think they initially turned us down. Even though we won the grand final, they said we couldn't come in because of the ground and probably other reasons, I don't know.

The chairman fought tooth and nail to get us in and they eventually they let us in. But without any funding. Every Super League club got so much money centrally but Wakefield didn't get any. They wouldn't share any of the money with us. That was disappointing, but beggars can't be choosers. We wanted to get into Super League, 'The Promised Land'.

I think everybody expected us to go down, but we went out and won 10 games early on. Lost the last 10, but it didn't matter. We got that magical 20 points and that kept us in Super League for another year. It was like the gold rush in America, frontier times for us financially. But it was just a great experience and we were all experiencing it together. We didn't really know if we were doing it right or wrong. But we were doing the best we could and we got those 10 wins.

[Becoming a full-time player was] everything I ever dreamed of. I was, at best, a decent player in the First Division, not great and certainly not the best, but I was alright. Going full-time made me as a player and gave me the opportunity to develop my skills, my strength and my speed. Going full-time I became a much better player than I ever could have been part-time.

[Before going full-time we trained] twice a week and Friday nights or Saturday mornings. I think they made it three times a week later on as the club progressed and they realised they needed more time with the players. No weights generally. Weights were something you took on in your own time. It was a bit of fitness on a Tuesday, ball skills and defence on Thursday and a final run through on Friday or Saturday.

It was a massive change and it took some getting to grips with. It took a few years for most Super League clubs to come to terms with what being full-time meant. Initially a lot of clubs kept the players too long at the club. They thought, "You're full-time you need to do nine to five" which doesn't really work in a sporting environment. It took a while, not just at Wakefield but for a few clubs, to come to terms with the fact that it was the quality of time that they are there, not the

166

quantity of time. It might be called full-time, but keeping them there for 40 hours a week is not really as beneficial as it could be. Two years down the line I think they had learnt that lesson.

I tore my cruciate that first year, so I was injured. But I much preferred playing in the summer. I think if you asked most players they would agree. There's nothing worse than playing at Thrum Hall on a December Sunday afternoon, it's ridiculous. Odsal as well – you go to Odsal and it's still cold. If you remember, the decision to go from winter to summer was buried beneath the decision to go to Super League. Super League was the bigger story. They decided to move from winter to summer at the same time and there wasn't too much said about that because everyone was complaining about the Super League concept and the teams merging. The summer/winter went through without debate because there was a bigger issue on the horizon, and rightly so for me, I think it's a better sport because of it.

In 1997 to 1998 I started an independent sports retail outlet. It was all right, but we learnt very quickly that JJB and the nationals had it sewn up. They were very, very small margins for us. We enjoyed it and it was good experience. But it was never going to give us the apartment in Marbella.

At that time we needed to develop an online shop and they were ridiculously expensive. We couldn't afford to pay someone. I did a bit of computing, so I went on to learn myself and from there we developed the business. It turns out there are a lot of small businesses like we were who can't access internet services, e-commerce, search engine marketing and all that, so I developed that side of things into a business.

I was never much for coffees in Starbucks or the Playstation which were popular with other players. There's a lot of time to fill as a player and I was always conscious that I was going to finish playing at some point and what was I going to do? Coaching was an option which I took with Hull KR, but there are only so many coaching jobs.

The company is called Buffalo, we call it Buffalo because it's my plan B. Rugby league chews you up and spits you out which it could do at any time. I always wanted to be self-sufficient so I knew I had some security. I enjoy it. It was a hobby that I did as a player and has developed and developed, and is getting too big for me now!
Francis Stephenson

Bramley: 'Here one day and gone the next'
Obviously losing your ground is a major blow to any team... you lose your spiritual home. I don't know the whole details because at that time I wasn't actively involved. But I think they had an offer from a company to build houses there, which on reflection was a huge mistake. If we were in dire straits, that really put the final nail in the coffin. After that we were on borrowed time. It is now a housing

estate, the old ground, although the pub is still there. Other than the road being named after the ground, McLaren Field, you would never know there's been a rugby club there.

So we left there probably in 1995 and went to play at Kirkstall, which was a rugby union ground. It wasn't a million miles from were we'd been, it's just a 15 or 20 minute walk down the hill into Kirkstall really. But it wasn't home. There was no feeling it was your ground. You felt like you were just transient... passing through.

We spent two or three years there before we moved up to Headingley and that was the kiss of death because we were seen as just the Leeds feeder team, which was absolutely not what we wanted to be. It was difficult rattling around in Headingley. When you've only got two or three hundred hardcore spectators it's a soulless place and we spent three years there before we folded in 1999. We just seemed to go out without so much as a whimper really. There were no businessmen to ride to the rescue, nothing from the Rugby Football League. We were here one day and gone the next.

[After the Bramley club folded] the supporters kept in touch. They used to have regular meetings at the Old Vic pub in Bramley and there was an awful lot of talk about what could be done. I wasn't privy to all the meetings that went on. But the bottom line was there was a desire and will to reinvent the club in some shape or other, whether it was playing amateur rugby league on a Sunday morning just to retain the name and have a team to follow or in the shape of a semi-professional team back in the National Leagues. But the problems were getting money, finding a ground to play on and all the logistical issues, and that's before you've got to find a coach and players to play. There were a number of sort of false dawns. There was a five-year period where there was no rugby played under the Bramley name [from 1999 to 2004].

People put an awful lot of time in. I wasn't in the area but kept in touch and we launched a scheme, where you could buy shares in the club at £50 a share and that was very successful. The likes of Jamie Peacock and Jamie Jones Buchanan contributed. They came from the Stanningley club. An awful lot of work had been done by the likes of Cliff Spracklen and Martin Chaney. They were the real driving force, the rest of us were just kept informed and did what we could. They were the real movers and shakers behind this idea of having a supporters' Co-operative team and to this day they still do an awful lot of work.

We rejoined the league in 2004. There had been talk about reforming a team for a couple of years. Martin and Cliff did an awful lot of that work and the negotiations in trying to find somewhere to play. It became apparent when the RFL launched the National League 3 in 2003, that would be the most likely way for us to get back into it and gave us something to aim for.

We didn't have a ground so we didn't meet any of the rugby league minimum standards that they had in place. Martin and Cliff looked at various grounds and there was talk about us going to Morley rugby union club. Farsley Celtic would have been an ideal place to play for many people because it's pretty adjacent to Bramley. They're an up-and-coming football team and they have the infrastructure at the ground, floodlights, corporate boxes, albeit on a lower level, but at the level we are looking at we don't need a grand stadium. I think Farsley were reluctant to accommodate us. They must have been because they have rebuffed us ever since.

It was Martin and Cliff's focus to try and get us into National League 3. There was no promotion or relegation between National League 3 and 2 because most of the clubs don't meet the standards the Rugby Football League set, but it was nevertheless a way to get back into rugby league football. In the off-season between September and April the following year we had a couple of pre-season friendlies. We got Phil Helliwell who used to play for Bradford on board as our coach and recruited the players, I would imagine, through contacts within the game, because a lot were predominantly amateur players who have got a pedigree within the amateur game either in Yorkshire or Lancashire. So they pulled a team together to start the 2004 season

It seems a bit sad to say, but [when the reformed club played its first game] it felt quite emotional really. It was exciting, probably a bit like Christmas when you are 10 or 11 years old. Five years doesn't seem like a long time. But it does when you haven't got a team to follow. I went to watch Leeds for five years and I still do occasionally. But I don't have the same affinity or the same emotional rollercoaster ride as I do watching Bramley. You can't just switch allegiances and I wouldn't want to.

We played Sheffield Hillsborough Hawks in our first game in May 2004. Graham Idle – our old player – came back and did the ceremonial kick-off. We had 1,200 spectators which was, and remains to this day a record crowd for that league.

It's hard to put into words, but you saw people you hadn't seen for a long time. In the 1970s nobody wore rugby shirts to rugby matches whereas it's quite a fashion thing now. But you had people coming out with old Bramley shirts, people seeing old friends again.

The result was almost immaterial, it would have been a fairytale to win, but fair credit to Sheffield they came back and scored about 10 points in the last 10 minutes to draw the game 14–14. It was a great day, 'we're back' and it was the start of something. We had an infrastructure, we had a team, a non-profit management committee made up of supporters, a coach who wanted to be there, we had 17 guys who turned up and were part of the team.

It was just a great day to be alive, to stand on the hill at Stanningley and watch your team play. To think "I'll need to get to know these guys now" and "next week we're playing wherever and the week after we're at home again" and "great, let's see where it takes us, where we can go from here."

I was happy that I could watch Bramley playing again. Now the team is in a comfortable position within the National League. I am committed to ensuring that Bramley's future remains secure, having become a board member, writing the match-day programme and yearbook, maintaining the club's statistics and writing match reports for the press.

Andy Coldrick

Making an impact in the community
I did a bit of work with my predecessor eight or nine years ago, Andy Harland. He was a development officer part-funded by the [Bradford] Bulls and the council. I'd helped out with the second team while I was at London. That was the only experience I had until I came back to live in Leeds when I was playing with Huddersfield and Hunslet.

Then he [Andy Harland] moved on and his post became vacant. Although I applied for it and got a lot of help from Andy, I didn't think I'd get the post, because I had a definite lack of qualifications. But I had some experience and I knew Bradford quite well, having played here for two years as a junior. So I knew the communities quite well and lo and behold I got the job.

At that time I stopped playing rugby and I must admit that I was glad to stop because week-in week-out it's on your mind to keep fit and stay fit, and then there are the pressures of when you're playing. But I consider myself very fortunate to still be involved in the game that I love.

I don't have an academic background, but I went to university and studied for a sports diploma at Leeds Met, which was a great help for me. I go back now and have a good relationship with people who were my tutors. Now, eight years on, I like to think that the projects we do are very effective and make an impact in the community.

I like the idea of working for the local authority because we do concentrate on communities with foundation work. Get them involved first, then provide them with pathways to mainstream. I'm not saying it's all the governing body is interested in, that would be a wrong thing to say. First and foremost it's about talent identification rather than participation, although that's beginning to change. My issue is that we're not engaging with ethnic communities as much as we should do, especially South Asian communities, hence why we formed BARA (British Asian Rugby Association).

That was really important and let me say, at this time, that rugby league has done more than any governing body. I know this because I work with other governing bodies. I sit on the national Asian football forum and we're still head-to-head with the FA about them making a

170

change. We've come out with two documents since I've been involved; *Asians can't play football*, and 10 years on we wrote another document. A wasted decade because the FA haven't really taken on board some of our points of view and our advice on how to take things forward.

But it does get frustrating that the city of Bradford has so much potential. We're doing as much as we can, but we could be doing more. I think it's fair to say that it's both sides of the coin. Our communities and other communities can do more for themselves as well. That's something that should have been highlighted by Government. But we could do a lot more to get them engaged. So we set up the British Asian Rugby Association to do that. Clearly we need some positive role models and we have a number of individuals who can work alongside these relevant governing bodies, local authorities, professional and amateur clubs to provide advice and guidance about how to engage people.

People were saying "there's not many Asians playing", but by forming the association we've been able to put a team together. I'm not sure if we've got the terminology of the association right. But it was important that we had something hard hitting that could make an impact. We've brought a few Asians back into the game because there's an association there. But it is inclusive and is an organisation which targets all sections of the community. Primarily we do look to engage with the disadvantaged communities, the isolated communities and the ones who have not been given opportunities. But purposely when we put a team together, we make sure that it is quite a diverse mix.

I was at the Rugby Parliamentary group and made a statement that our national teams whether it be rugby league, football or cricket should represent the diverse communities that live work and play in the country. That's not happening because you have these issues and that's why kids won't take part in sports. We were lucky because we had a very responsive mechanism within our family unit and close family friends. I'm not saying we're any different from anybody else, but individually we were determined to succeed. But it's not so easy for other people to do that.

I keep making statements that we can guarantee participation. But what I can't guarantee is filtering these boys and girls into mainstream clubs and to be retained. We have an issue of retainment anyway regardless of who they are. But in particular the Asian communities and I've made it clear to both governing bodies [the RFL and RFU] that they need to go through an educational development programme raising awareness about different cultures, religions etc. It won't be the answer, but it will help provide more understanding of the needs of these different communities. Also we need prolonged delivery in these communities. Small projects are no good. We do that very well, but we don't continue it. I think that there's still a lot of learning and education to be done on both sides.

You don't have to be Asian to go into the Asian community you can be from any background. You just need to do your homework well and have an understanding of who you are working with. We've got so much to offer and it's not just the South Asian communities, we've also got European communities. Leeds also has a strong Arab and Iraqi presence. So if we haven't capitalised on these Asian communities how are we going to capitalise on the other communities? If you look at the amateur clubs who are in need of volunteers, there's a massive pool out there who, if welcomed in right way, would love to help out and take part. So I think we're missing out on a big chunk of resources at no cost to us apart from making them feel welcome.

Ikram Butt

'People who stick together'

Look at the way the amateur game reacted with me [after I broke my neck playing in a match in 1995]. They did a year's worth of fundraising. The proper rugby league is the amateur game because that's where you find the people who stick together. When I had my accident, Dewsbury Moor RLFC did a sponsored walk from Dewsbury to Leeds.

Your parents at the side of the ground, taking you there, taking you back, running you here, running you there. Parents would have done it for kids who were going to have no future in rugby league whatsoever, but they loved the game and their parents loved the game so they got them involved. You can go to Greetland on a freezing cold Sunday and you know your parents are there, you feel part of the team and you're made to feel great. The whole rugby league, everybody who is involved in a certain capacity knows what they're doing and knows what it is all about. It's the things which are, I suppose higher up which you look at and think that's wrong.

I was 17 [when I had my accident] and had a few mates who had signed (as professionals). The bloke who was our manager was good friends with James Lowes. So James Lowes would do a load of press with me and things like that. John Bastion was coaching me at the time and a load of lads from Featherstone; Chris Burton and Ikram Butt came into hospital. He got Paul Newlove to come over and I spent an hour with him talking. All of which players didn't have to do. In football it's written into their contracts that they have to do six hours community work etc. whereas rugby league players then, if something had happened to somebody, they would have a do at a rugby club. Stanningley would put on a do or you'd go to somewhere else where they would put on a night for you and all the proceeds would go to you. Through the [RFL] Benevolent Fund you would meet other people it happened to and they've had similar things done for them.

Because the Benevolent Fund only got set up a couple of years ago, there was separate fundraising for me. They set up my own benefit fund at the time and did stuff from shaving their hair off, to bungee jumping, to walking from Dewsbury to Leeds. Anything that could have been done was done by the people involved in the rugby club. It's weird because I got a breakdown of every single thing which was sent. It's about two years since I last looked at it and I remember looking at some of the names of people who sent things. A cheque from Ray French, I remember seeing that. You'd have cards from clubs who were your biggest enemies, 'get-well-soon' cards. I remember them having a load of badges made up for me 'I support Killer' badges and some of the Leeds team from the Challenge Cup wore them on their tracksuits.

Nobody had to do anything and it shows when something bad does happen that rugby league does come together in a way which I don't suppose many other sports would be like, with the craic and everything that goes with it.

Paul Kilbride

'One game, that's all it took'

Basically, Richard was taking Natalie our daughter [to watch a Bradford Bulls match]. I wasn't going to sit at home. So I went along and that's all it took, one game. I think it might have been against Leeds and you'd got the 'Awesome Foursome', and the two Paul brothers, who just made the game look so easy. I was lucky because I started going just when the Bulls were up there and also at the time when the rivalry between Bradford and Leeds, and Bradford and St Helens was very vocal, but there was never any physical nastiness.

The one thing that sticks in my mind is how we used to get up to Odsal well before the start of the pre-match entertainment because it was so good. You really wanted to be there. These days you've got people hanging around in the bars before they come into the stands. Back then they were in the stands for the start of the pre-match entertainment. I mean some of the acts they've had up at Odsal are just unbelievable. It was just quality entertainment and I think the whole mascot thing as well – Bullman and Bullboy – it really started to build and engage with the kids as well. It was fantastic. You really, really did look forward to going up there for a game day. Not just for the game itself, but for the whole experience.

Gill Johnson

Forming the Rugby League Disabled Supporters Association

Gill: When my disability started to kick in and cause issues, of course we started to look at things a bit differently. We used to travel to away games as well and a lot of the time it was just absolutely terrible as a

173

wheelchair user. You were lucky if you had a view of the game. You were very fortunate if your carer was anywhere near you.

Richard: People weren't aware there were problems and in 2004 we looked at setting up a Rugby League Disabled Supporters Association. In 2005 we actually saw the RFL and said "Look can we work with you and the clubs to get this association up and running", because the Disability Discrimination Act was coming in.

Gill: Looking at the conditions that rugby league fans were experiencing and then looking at the DDA there was just this huge gulf. The one thing that we didn't want was to see rugby league dragged through the mud. So our aim was to start the association and work with the rugby league to even things up so we didn't have cases of discrimination going to court. That's how it all started.

That's the thing about rugby league, once you start watching you get involved and get a passion for it. Before you know where you are it's become part of your life and you don't want to see negative press about it.

The RFL received the initiative really well. At the time Steve Fairhurst was the ethics and equality officer and I remember him openly saying to me "we need help". So they very much took everything on board. A lot of the codes of conduct the RFL have now started life with us and the Disabled Supporters Association. We work with the Rugby League Ground Safety Officers Association, which is great because they're the people that are really on the front line with regards to the safety of spectators and the whole viewing attitude. If you talk to those people and get them onside you've done the bulk of the work.

Odsal was a good example. We spent a lot of time talking to Bradford, it's our home club and they wanted to know what they could do and what they needed to do. As a result we got the level concourse – the viewing area right across the back of the main stand so you're completely out of the weather.

Gill: Steve Fairhurst had a chat with us and said "is there any chance you can go along to this?" It was a disability sports day at South Leeds Stadium and as usual we said "yes, we'll go along and have a look". Being a wheelchair user myself, suddenly seeing these guys playing rugby league in wheelchairs I thought was fantastic. From then on we got involved straight away.

Richard: It was started in France in 2000 by Wally Salvan and Robert Fassolette. They pushed it over in France and in 2004/5, did a tour of England and had a few demonstration games. It got picked up by some people and out of that we had two teams, Halifax and Wigan & District. It was still relatively new over here.

Gill: I remember saying to Richard "we've got to do something with this."

Richard: We got together at the World Club Challenge 2007 at the Reebok [Stadium], at Bolton. We were asked if we'd take it under the RLDSA umbrella and said "yes". Then in April there was a committee formed for the British Wheelchair Tag Rugby Association.

Gill: They have really serious issues [in France]. Unlike the RFL, the French Rugby League has not adopted this game as a derivative. They've adopted what is termed wheelchair rugby, but it isn't. The game's played with a round ball and [it] can be passed in any direction. It's also known as murderball in America and Canada. But it's being included in the 2012 Paralympics and that is why [the French Rugby League] is adopting it, so they can build their profile up.

Richard: It's hugely different. The rugby league version is played with a size 4 oval ball, you've got to pass it backwards and basically it is rugby league. The defensive line is four metres back and it's played on a 40 metre by 20 metre pitch, when we can find somewhere that big! There are five players on the pitch, five substitutes for a club game. Its rolling substitutions. But for an international it follows the rugby league: 12 substitutions, we play for 80 minutes.

Gill: The biggest difference I think that people would notice, apart from the fact that these guys are tearing about in chairs, is that each player wears a tag on their shoulder and if you lift the tag up and drop it, it's the equivalent of a tackle. The ball has then got to touch the floor and be passed.

Gill and Richard Johnson

"Beyond imagining"
The 2008 Wheelchair Tag Rugby World Cup
Gill: I think the RFL started to think this [Wheelchair Tag Rugby] was actually quite good, the first time we played at Brunel. That was 2008, an England against France international again. We'd struggled financially; it was fundraising right up to the last minute. But we managed to get enough money to put it on and it tied in with Champion Schools. We had a lot of representatives there from the RFL and we'd pushed and pushed for them to take an interest and that's when they did.

It was after that game that we first put it to them that there was an opportunity here because we'd been asked to take a team to Australia. Basically I'd sent our apologies, because there was just no way could we raise that amount of money. But we put it to the RFL and they took it up. AXA Insurance put up the money for flights for the team and the RFL met the rest of the costs and provided the kit. The team played in exactly the same kit as the running game and we went out there and did the unbelievable, won every game we played.

[We got the go ahead] about six weeks before. It's one of the most stressful times we've ever had, but the end-product was beyond imagining really. It was so worthwhile.

175

Richard: New Zealand felt they couldn't do the country justice and withdrew, which left us with only three teams, England, France and Australia and it ended up with a Barbarian representative side that made the four countries up to make it an official World Cup rather than just a Tri-Nations.

Gill: We had to base the team on the team that played in the [2008 England versus France] international, because we just didn't have the time to do a selection process. We appointed Phil Roberts as the England coach, who's an amazing guy. He coaches the Wigan club and I think that's one of the best things we did. He took the team and it made my job so much easier, because before I was the manager, the kit man, the physio. I was all these different things. Richard was refereeing and it took so much pressure off me to finally have a coach that knew what a coach should do and just got on with it.

We met up to set off at Birch Services and we were all there in the early hours of the morning. None of us had slept; we were wide awake because nobody had been on a long haul flight before. We travelled down to Heathrow and flew out from there into Singapore and then to Sydney. There were banks of snow either side of the motorway when we were leaving and when we arrived in Sydney it was 30 to 40 degree heat. We stayed most of the time at the Sydney Academy of Sport which is where Manly are based and it was awe inspiring, because you quite often get the players dropping in. We played at Carrageen, we played at Liverpool and went over to Newcastle, Mount Druitt and we won every match.

Richard: It was a round-robin, then a semi-final and a final. With winning all the group games we were top and played the Barbarian representative side and won that quite easily. Obviously they'd only got together quite recently. But they played their hearts out. That was their final and they loved every minute of it. Then it was France against Australia which was a bit of a surprise; France were defeated I think it was 28–24.

Gill: It was the first time ever that there'd been any fisticuffs at a wheelchair tag rugby game. It got heated. We just got the England squad out and myself and Richard were talking to the French players because they were in a group and absolutely heartbroken. It was more senior members of the French entourage that were involved.

Richard: We beat Australia in the final at Mount Druitt 44–12.

Gill: Something I remember vividly and will do for the rest of my life is the point we actually won, it was just surreal. I just remember bursting into tears and I saw one of the players disappear out of the door and thought where's he going, because it was one of the younger players. So I had to make sure he was OK. He'd gone out to ring his mum and he was talking absolutely deadpan as if the worst had happened. All I can remember him saying is "we've won" and all I could hear was screaming from the other end of the phone.

as a player walks through the doors, they're all excited. Obviously for the players to tell them to work hard at school it has a bigger impact than just me saying it. So from that aspect it works really well. They also come in for the celebration events. Each group has a celebration event at the end of the ten weeks and the players give out the prizes.

The players that we've had, you don't have to give them a lot of direction. They're in there straight away. They sit down with the kids and just get on with it really. So we've been lucky from that view point. Some of them are a bit nervous, some of the younger ones we get, they haven't had a lot of experience dealing with kids. But they've been really good the ones we've had so far. We get quite a mix, some of the more experienced players, but it tends to be the younger ones because the club wants to give them some experience, you know, going out there, dealing with kids and the public. So I think it helps them out a little bit as well.

Black and ethnic involvement in rugby league, I think is the full title [of a] new project brought out by the RFL this year. They're wanting to launch a website to celebrate the kind of diversity of backgrounds in rugby league to coincide with Black History Month. So what the RFL wanted from all the rugby clubs was profiles of past and present players and staff from ethnic minority backgrounds. So we decided it was a really good project and we could tie it in with the media projects that we run. Basically we got players and staff from the Giants from different minority backgrounds to come in and our pupils got the opportunity to interview them about their cultural background and their heritage and find out about their rugby careers, their personal lives, find out if they suffered any racism playing rugby league. So I think it was really great project for our kids, a good eye opener for them. I think it was good for the players as well to give them an opportunity to tell the kids about their background and where they came from.

Like I said I try to go as much as I can so I can up my knowledge on the rules of the game and stuff I don't know all the rules yet but I'm getting there. I really enjoy it. I enjoy the kind of contact and it's really fast paced and really exciting. Eorl Crabtree, not only is he a great player, but we've had him in come in a couple of our sessions and he's absolutely fantastic with the kids. He's a really nice guy and Michael Lawrence, again, he's one that is a regular visitor at the study centre, he's really great with the kids as well.
Navjit Uppal

Appendix 1: The contributors

John Atkinson: After playing rugby league at school John played rugby union for Roundhay before becoming a professional rugby league player with Leeds in 1965. He spent 17 years at Headingley, scoring 340 tries in 512 appearances. He won the Challenge Cup three times and the Championship twice before moving on for a short spell as player-coach with Carlisle. He also made 38 international appearances, was a member of the Great Britain team which won the World Cup Final in 1972 and went on four tours to Australia and New Zealand, including the successful 1970s Lions tour.

Maurice Bamford: Maurice grew up a stone's throw from Headingley and was taken to watch Leeds by his father just after the Second World War. He played rugby league in the local schools competition and signed as a professional with Hull in 1953 before moving on to Dewsbury in 1957. After a spell in local amateur rugby league during the mid-1960s he began a remarkable coaching career which reached its peak with a three year spell as Great Britain coach in the mid-1980s. In all Maurice coached 12 professional clubs, including Leeds, Wigan, and Bramley, as well as a host of amateur sides. He also worked as a rugby league development officer for Leeds City Council and has recently had published a number of popular books on the game.

David Barends: David made his mark playing in the 'coloured' rugby union competitions around Cape Town in the 1960s. Denied the opportunity to progress his career by the apartheid regime, he signed for Wakefield Trinity in 1970. He moved onto York in 1973 before joining Bradford Northern where he was an integral part of the team which won back-to-back championships in 1980 and 1981. In 1979 he became the first foreign born player to represent Great Britain.

Doris Beard: Doris became assistant to club secretary Eric England at Bradford Northern in 1954. By 1960 she had taken over the role as secretary, becoming the first female to occupy the position in professional rugby league.

John Beaumont John has supported Huddersfield Rugby League Club since his early childhood when he spent many hours at Fartown with and family friend Hubert Pogson and some of the club's other former players such as Ben Gronow. He followed the Huddersfield throughout the club's decline in the 1980s, travelling all over England and even into Europe.

Keith Bell: Following in the footsteps of his father who played for Featherstone and later worked as a groundsman with the club, Keith signed as a professional at Post Office Road in the late 1960s. He stayed with the club until 1990, winning both the Championship and Challenge Cup before finishing his career with a two year spell at Hunslet.

Jackie Blackburn: After watching Featherstone Rovers and playing schoolboy rugby league Jackie signed as a professional at Post Office Road in 1939 and played against Wakefield in the clubs Yorkshire Cup Final victory later that season. He stayed at Featherstone throughout his career which ended in the 1950s and later served on the club committee.

Eddie Bottomley: Eddie became assistant secretary of the Rugby Football League in 1952. Over the next two decades he worked closely with RFL secretary Bill Fallowfield during a period in which the game began to change significantly. He retired in 1979, five years after David Oxley had taken over the administration of the game, and died in 2008.

Alan Bradford: After beginning his amateur career with Overthorpe under-13s Alan moved on to Thornhill Boys Club, Dewsbury Boys and Shaw Cross. He also represented the Dewsbury District team. He had a brief spell in the professional game with Halifax and coached the Thornhill Lees club when his playing days had finished.

Keith Bridges: Keith watched Featherstone Rovers as a boy and after playing rugby union at Normanton Grammar school joined the club as a professional when just 17. Arguably the leading hooker in the game during the 1970s and 1980s, he won the Championship four times and the Challenge Cup twice during spells with Featherstone, Bradford Northern and Hull. He also played three times for Great Britain and eight times for England.

Keith Burhouse: A lifelong Huddersfield supporter, Keith stepped up to play a vital role in keeping the club alive during the 1980s, working tirelessly at the decaying Fartown ground when its fortunes declined sharply. In recognition of his contribution to the club he was made an associate director in 1989 and after witnessing Huddersfield's renaissance in the 1990s he proudly still holds that position today.

Alf Burnell: Another graduate of the famous Hunslet schools rugby league competition, Alf signed for the Parkside club after serving as a submariner the Second World War. He played his entire career with Hunslet, also representing Yorkshire and Great Britain, with whom he toured Australia in 1954, before retiring in 1958. His involvement with the club continued in various roles, including groundsman, coach, and director when his playing days were over.

Ikram Butt: A boyhood Leeds fan Ikram joined older brother Tony as a professional with the club in 1987. After representing England Colts he moved on to Featherstone and then London Broncos, having become England's first full Muslim rugby international in either code during his time at Featherstone. After spells with Huddersfield and Hunslet, Ikram retired and took up a development role in the game, initially with Bradford Council. In 2002 he formed the British Asian Rugby Association (BARA) and in 2008 received an award for his work with the organisation at the Muslim Honours ceremony.

Graham Chalkley: Graham grew up in Sharlston and played as an amateur for the village's famous club. He signed as a professional with Batley in the late 1960s and later moved on to Dewsbury. He has also researched and written a history of Sharlston Rovers which was published by London League Publications Ltd in 2006.

Morris and Harry Child: The Child brothers have watched rugby league since the 1930s. Although supporters of local club Dewsbury, they also witnessed some of the games most famous matches including the 1954 Challenge Cup final replay at Odsal.

Andy Coldrick: Andy began watching Bramley as a schoolboy in the late 1960s. Despite embarking on a career in the RAF, he remained a staunch supporter throughout the club's subsequent decline and eventual demise in the late 1990s. In 2004 he was present at the inaugural match of Bramley Buffaloes and is now more actively involved with the club.

Phil Crabtree: After making a handful of 'A' team appearances while home on leave during National Service, Phil signed for Bradford Northern when he left the armed forces. He enjoyed a 13 year career at Odsal which came to a sad end as the club folded in 1963, before being reformed in the following year.

Ken Dean: When he came out of the armed forces in 1948, Ken joined Halifax after playing just a handful of matches with local amateur club Greetland. Over the next decade he was cornerstone of the great Halifax side that just missed out on major honours, appearing in two Yorkshire Cup Finals, three Championship Finals, two Challenge Cup Finals at Wembley and the famous 1954 Challenge Cup Final replay at Odsal.

Bak Diabira: Although he grew up and enjoyed a successful amateur career in Hull, Bak signed for Bradford in the mid-1960s. He spent nine years at Odsal where he built a reputation as one of the game's most inventive half-backs before moving on for a brief spell with New Hunslet, following which he retired through injury. Bak later returned to the game with Blackpool Borough, where he became player-coach, and ended his career with a stint in the same role at Keighley during the early 1980s.

Malcolm Dixon: Malcolm signed as a professional with Featherstone Rovers in 1955 and spent 16 years at Post Office Road before ending his career with York. He made three international appearances, one for England and two for Great Britain. In 1967 he captained the Featherstone side which won the Challenge Cup at Wembley.

John Downes: A regular at Odsal since his childhood, John has also worked for the Bradford Bulls Community Development Department. He was heritage officer for the 'Bulls Heritage Project' and has been closely involved in the successful bid which secured Heritage Lottery Funding for the clubs 'Past Times' project in 2010.

Albert Eyre: Albert was one of the few players to come through the Hunslet schoolboy system and when he turned professional did not do so at Parkside. Instead, he joined Keighley before moving on to Leeds where, along with his brother Ken, he was part of the club's successful side in the late 1960s.

Trevor Foster: After joining the club from Newport RUFC in 1938, Trevor played 428 games for Bradford Northern and won the Challenge Cup three times. He also played 16 times for Wales, three times for Great Britain and was a member of the historic 1946 Indomitables touring party to Australia and New Zealand. After retiring as a player in 1955, Trevor was instrumental in the resurrection of Bradford Northern following its collapse in 1963. He continued his association with the club enjoying its success in the Super League era as timekeeper at matches until his death in 2005. He was awarded an MBE in 2001 and inducted into the

Welsh Sports Hall of Fame in 2004. A biography of Trevor was published in 2005, just before he died.

Peter Fox: The oldest of the three famous rugby league playing brothers from Sharlston, Peter's playing career began with the local amateur club before playing as a professional for Featherstone Rovers, Batley, Hull KR and Wakefield Trinity. He then spent more than 20 years as a coach in the professional game leading Bradford Northern to two championships and winning the Challenge Cup with Featherstone Rovers. He also spent time at Leeds, Wakefield Trinity and Bramley, where he achieved promotion for one of Yorkshire's less successful clubs. He also coached Yorkshire, England and Great Britain. A biography of Peter was published in 2008.

Carl Gibson: A former schoolboy rugby union international, Carl signed for hometown club Batley in 1981 where he broke into the Great Britain side before moving to Leeds in 1986. While at Headingley he became a Great Britain regular, making two tours to the southern hemisphere in 1988 and 1990. Carl moved on to Featherstone in 1993 and retired after a brief second spell with Batley.

David Gronow: Grandson of Huddersfield great Ben Gronow, rugby league has always been part of David's life. He watched his father and uncles who also played for Huddersfield and played himself as an amateur. He has also served as secretary of the Huddersfield Past Players Association and has recently had published two books on the club's history.

Geoff Gunney: Geoff signed as a professional for Hunslet in 1951. He subsequently made 569 appearances for his local club, including the 1959 Championship and 1965 Challenge Cup Finals. He also made 11 appearances for Great Britain, including as a British Lion to Australia and New Zealand in 1954, and in the 1957 World Cup. He captained Hunslet in last ever match at Parkside and was instrumental in the formation of New Hunslet immediately after the original club folded in 1973.

Cora Haley: Cora married into rugby league family. Her husband was chairman of Overthorpe Rangers and she took on the job of secretary in 1949, becoming the only woman to occupy that role in the Dewsbury and District League. Cora gave up the post when she became pregnant in 1953.

Len Haley: Len began his career playing amateur rugby league in the Dewsbury area and then played rugby union in the armed forces. When his National Service ended he stayed in the XV-a-side code with Cleckheaton, but soon turned professional with Bradford Northern and became a first team regular during the 1950s.

Derek Hallas: A product of the Hunslet schools rugby league system, Derek joined Roundhay rugby union club after playing the XV-a-side game in the armed forces during national service. He signed as a professional in rugby league with Keighley in 1953. Six years later he joined Leeds where in 1961 he scored two tries in the club's first ever championship success. Following another brief spell with Keighley he moved to Australian club Parramatta and later coached Halifax.

Fred Halliday: Fred grew up watching his father Cyril playing for Huddersfield. An England international, Cyril played for Huddersfield and Keighley during the inter-war period. He died in 2009.

Karl Harrison: Karl began his rugby league playing career as an amateur with Drighlington and played rugby union at school in Morley. He turned professional with Featherstone Rovers and also had spells with Hull and Halifax. He played 14 times for Great Britain and 6 times for England before moving into coaching. After a spell as assistant coach with the Bradford Bulls he was appointed head coach at Salford in 2002 where he spent five years. He became head coach of Batley in 2009, and led them to a memorable Northern Rail Cup win in 2010, the club's first major trophy since the 1952–53 season.

Chris Hawksworth: Chris watched Featherstone Rovers as a boy before becoming a journalist covering the local rugby league scene for the *Pontefract and Castleford Express* during the 1960s. He has since worked in radio and television for the BBC.

John Henderson: Born in Maryport in 1929, John fulfilled his boyhood ambition by joining local club Workington in 1950, where he spent five seasons playing under the legendry Gus Risman. After touring Australia and New Zealand with Great Britain in 1954 he joined Halifax before moving on to York in 1958 and retiring a year later.

David Hinchliffe: David grew up watching the great Wakefield Trinity team of the 1960s. He also played local amateur rugby league and after becoming MP for Wakefield in 1987 formed the All-Party Parliamentary Rugby League Group. He campaigned on many issues about the game in parliament, including the right to play rugby league in the armed forces. He stood down as an MP in 2005, having been a well-respected chair of the Health Select Committee. Since then he has remained involved in the game, and is a trustee of the Rugby League Benevolent Fund. He wrote an account of his work for the game in Parliament, *Rugby's Class War*, which was published by London League Publications Ltd in 2000.

Phil Hodgson: A lifelong Hunslet supporter, after playing amateur rugby league Phil embarked on a career as journalist with the *Rugby Leaguer* newspaper in the early 1990s. He has since had published a number of books on the game and become a popular writer with various rugby league newspapers and magazines. He now writes a weekly column for *League Express*, and is still heavily involved in the amateur game.

Donald Hunt: Donald played rugby union while growing up in Ireland. After serving in the armed forces during the Second World War he took a farm in Featherstone and became involved with the local rugby league club joining the committee at Post Office road during the 1970s. He has written two books about the club.

Eddie Illingworth: After enjoying success as a soccer player during his national service in the army, Eddie turned to rugby league when he returned to civilian life. He joined Batley and although mostly alternating between the first team and the 'A' enjoyed a 10 year career with the club.

David Ingham: David began watching local club Keighley while a boy in the late 1940s and has been a fan of the game ever since. He spent time as a player and administrator in local amateur rugby league and regularly attended the game's major domestic and international matches. In 1988 and 1992 he and his wife followed the Lions tour to Australia.

Roger Ingham: Unusually for a Dalesman from Skipton, Roger is a lifelong fan of rugby league. He watched Keighley as boy and has been a regular at the game's major occasions since the 1950s, attending most of the big matches which pulled huge crowds to Odsal during that decade. Also a successful fell runner, Roger met many of the game's stars when they competed at rural sports meetings.

Harry Jepson: Harry grew up in Hunslet and first visited Parkside during the 1920s. After the Second World War he became secretary of the famous Hunslet Schools Rugby League Association and also assistant secretary of Hunslet Rugby League Club. He was promoted to secretary at Parkside in 1963, before moving to work for Leeds seven years later. Harry became football director at Headingley in the 1980s and is now club president. He led the team out at Wembley for the 2010 Challenge Cup Final. He has also served on the Rugby Football League board of directors and was awarded an OBE for his services to the game.

Gill and Richard Johnson: Richard grew up watching Bradford Northern and began taking his wife Gill and daughter Natalie to Odsal in the early 2000s. As a wheelchair user Gill's concerns about the disabled facilities at most grounds led to them forming the Rugby League Disabled Supporters Association in 2005. In 2007, they became involved in wheelchair rugby league. Gill, as team manager, and Richard as a referee, were part of the victorious England party in the 2008 World Cup.

Paul Kilbride: Paul grew up watching Leeds in the 1980s and played rugby league at school. As a teenager he represented Leeds City boys. But his career was tragically cut short in 1995 when he snapped his spinal cord playing in a match. Paul received great support from many people involved in both the amateur and professional game and has since worked to help promote the Rugby League Benevolent fund.

John Kitson: John's family has a strong background in rugby league. His grandfather George played for Halifax when the Northern Union was formed in 1895 and led the club to Championship and Challenge Cup success during the 1902–03 season. His father and uncles also played for the Halifax and although John's own career was cut short by injury when having trials at Thrum Hall, he has continued to support them ever since.

Linda Kitson: Linda has childhood memories of watching Halifax in the 1950s and remembers stars such as Johnny Freeman who lived nearby. She has continued to support the club and after providing sponsorship while running the Woolpack Inn, Linda and her husband John got involved with the supporters' trust.

Bryn Knowelden: After his hopes of a career in football were dashed by the start of the Second World War, Bryn began playing rugby league while working in the Barrow shipyards. He soon signed for the local club and was then picked to go on the 1946 Indomitables tour to Australia and New Zealand. On his return he moved to Warrington and won the Championship in 1948 and the Challenge Cup in 1950 before ending his career with Hull Kingston Rovers.

Jack Merewood: Born in 1919, as a boy Jack was taken to watch Huddersfield by his father. He served in the army during the Second World War and upon returning from the conflict followed the great Huddersfield side of the 1940s.

Mick Morgan: Although brought up in Featherstone watching his cousin Arnie play at Post Office Road, Mick signed as a professional with Wakefield Trinity in 1965. He later had spells with Carlisle and Oldham before finishing his career playing in the 'A' team with Castleford at the age of 44. He also played six times for England, won the Man of Steel award in 1982 and has worked for Castleford in the commercial department since the late 1980s.

Sam Morton: Sam first played rugby league at school. He joined Dewsbury Celtic in 1958 and over the next few decades served as player, secretary and manager as the club won the Yorkshire Cup in 1974 and 1977 and qualified to face Wigan in the first round proper of the Challenge Cup in 1978. He also coached the first BARLA tour to Papua New Guinea, Australia and New Zealand in 1978 and is now manager of the George Hotel Rugby League Heritage Centre.

Garfield Owen: After winning six caps for Wales at rugby union, Garfield Owen signed as a professional with Halifax in 1956. He also won a cap for Wales at rugby league before moving on to Keighley in 1961. He retired in 1965 and was inducted into the Halifax Hall of Fame in 1993.

Stanley Pickles: A lifelong Leeds supporter, Stanley first remembers going to a match at Headingley in 1915. He has remained a supporter of the club ever since and was a regular throughout the 1920s and 1930s. He vividly remembers the big matches and star players of that time.

Bev Risman: Part of a famous rugby league family, his father Gus being one of the game's legends and his brother John having played as a professional for many years, Bev won his first honours in rugby union as an England international and British Lion before signing for Leigh in 1961. He joined Leeds in 1966and switched to playing at full-back. He kicked four goals in the final to win the Challenge Cup for Leeds in 1968, and was part of the team that won the Championship in 1969. In 1968, he captained Great Britain in the 1968 World Cup, making him one of the few dual-code Lions. He retired as a player in 1970, following a knee injury. He subsequently played a major role in setting up Student Rugby League, did youth development work for the London Broncos, and helped set up the Rugby League Conference. He became the President of the RFL in 2010, the first person to be appointed to this post who was not a member of the RFL Council, a fitting honour to reflect a lifetime's service to the game.

Sid Rookes: Yet another former Hunslet schoolboy player, Sid signed at as a professional at Parkside in 1937. He worked at the AVRO factory in Yeadon during the war and had a spell on loan with Leeds after the Hunslet club closed down. But when activities resumed at Parkside in 1944, Sid returned to the club and spent eight more years with Hunslet before retiring.

Ken Senior: Ken played amateur rugby league in Huddersfield before signing professional forms at Fartown in 1962. During a 17 year career with the club he made 468+6 appearances for Huddersfield, scored 212 tries, represented Great Britain twice and played for Yorkshire. His appearances total for Huddersfield is only beaten by Douglas Clark. He has played a major role in the Huddersfield Past Players Association for many years, having first been elected chairman in 1985.

John Sheridan: After playing school and amateur rugby league in Castleford John signed as a professional with the local club after completing his national service in the mid-1950s. When injury ended his playing career in the mid-1960s he moved into coaching, initially with the Castleford 'A' team before spells as a head coach at Doncaster and Hunslet.

Bernard Shooman: Bernard has enjoyed a remarkable lifelong involvement in rugby league. A boyhood Leeds fan, he had long career as a player and coach with various clubs in the Leeds area, including Middleton Juniors, West Yorkshire Foundries and Stanningley. He has refereed in both the amateur and professional games. During the 1980s he was also secretary of the Dewsbury club and had a spell as a scout for Leeds. He has also served as chairman of the Leeds and District Amateur Rugby League.

Neil Shuttleworth: A lifelong Huddersfield supporter, Neil first watched the club during its successful spell in the immediate post war years. He became more closely involved in the 1980s, stepping in to help run the club after it almost went out of existence.

Tommy Smales: After watching hometown club Castleford as a boy Tommy played local schoolboy rugby league before signing for Featherstone Rovers in the mid-1950s. He then moved on to Huddersfield where he won the Championship in 1962 and after a spell with Bradford Northern signed for Australian side North Sydney. He also played eight times for Great Britain and coached at various clubs, winning the Challenge Cup in 1970 during his spell at Castleford.

Brian Smith: A boyhood fan of local club Keighley Brian worked as a journalist with the *Keighley News* and began reporting on rugby league in the early 1960s. In 1968 he became rugby league correspondent for the *Bradford Telegraph & Argus* and covered Bradford Northern and the game in general throughout the 1970s, 1980s and 1990s.

Geoff Smith: A lifelong Castleford fan, Geoff began watching the game in the 1940s. He has since become more closely involved with the club, working as a volunteer fundraiser and serving on the committee of the Past Players Association.

Francis Stephenson: The son of former professional player Nigel Stephenson, Francis enjoyed a successful junior career before signing for one of his father's old club Wakefield Trinity in 1993. While at Belle Vue he won promotion to Super League in 1998 and was selected for England's World Cup squad in 2000 before moving on to Wigan, London Broncos and Hull Kingston Rovers. Francis is now the operational manager at Wakefield Trinity Wildcats.

Mick Sullivan: Mick began playing rugby league for the Dewsbury based Shaw Cross Boys Club before signing with Huddersfield at the age of 18. In 1954 he made the first of his record 46 appearances for Great Britain in the inaugural World Cup tournament. He moved to Wigan in 1957 where he won two Challenge Cup Finals and a Championship Final. Mick also toured Australia and New Zealand with the successful 1958 and 1962 Lions and won the World Cup for a second time in 1960. He also had spells with St Helens, York, Doncaster and Dewsbury before his playing career ended.

Billy Thompson: One of the sport's great characters, from the late 1960s to the early 1980s Billy was among the world's leading rugby league referees. He took charge of the Championship Final twice, three Challenge Cup Finals at Wembley, three Premiership Finals and 11 Lancashire Cup finals. He also officiated in three World Cup competitions, including the Final of the 1977 tournament at the Sydney Cricket Ground, and three Great Britain test matches against Australia.

Stan Timmins: Stan came to the attention of various professional clubs while playing rugby union in the army. He signed for Wakefield Trinity in the late 1970s and moved into coaching and conditioning when still a player at Belle Vue. He moved on to take up similar roles with Sheffield Eagles, Hunslet, Castleford and Leeds Rhinos when his playing days had ended before embarking on an academic career, studying for PhD on race, racism and ethnicity in rugby.

Navjit Uppal: Navjit became interested in rugby league after going to watch the Huddersfield Giants with her sister. At the time she was working as a centre assistant at the Huddersfield Town Study Centre. But when a similar job became available with the Giants through the Playing for Success scheme, she applied for and got the post. Navjit currently works with groups of 9 to 15 year old students on a wide variety of after school projects at the Giants study centre.

Frank Wagstaff: Frank began his playing career with Kippax in 1934 before signing for Hunslet and then moving on to Castleford shortly before the Second World War broke out. Frank worked in a reserved occupation as a miner and although Castleford closed down, he continued to play throughout the conflict, appearing for Huddersfield, Keighley and Batley in the wartime competition. After the war he moved on to Featherstone, Rochdale and Huddersfield before ending his career with Batley. Frank died in 2008.

Joe Warham: Born in Warrington in 1920, Joe has been involved in rugby league for well over 60 years. After a playing career with Oldham and Swinton, he became coach at Rochdale before joining Leeds in 1958. He spent over 50 years at Headingley, leading the club to its first two championship titles as coach before taking up a managerial role. He became general manager of the club in 1980 and even after his retirement in 1990 has served as president of the Leeds Taverners Club and the Leeds ex-players' association.

Trevor Ward: The son of Bradford Northern and Great Britain captain Ernest, Trevor grew up watching his father play. After playing rugby league as a schoolboy he embarked on a career in rugby union with Wakefield and Halifax before signing as a professional with Wakefield Trinity in the mid-1960s. Trevor later moved to Dewsbury, but injury and the demands of his career as a fine art illustrator forced him to retire.

Harry Waring: Harry was born a stone's throw from the Dewsbury's Crown Flatt ground and his father and grandfather both supported the club and grew up watching the club when his uncle Eddie, the famous broadcaster and journalist, was team manager during the Second World War.

Frank Watson: Frank played schools rugby league in Hunslet in the 1930s and signed as a professional at Parkside in 1940. He moved across the city to Leeds in 1949 and after six years in the first team became player-coach for the 'A' team before taking up a similar role at Batley in 1957.

Ronnie Wolfenden: Ronnie was a boyhood fan of local club Halifax in the 1930s and also played local amateur rugby league. He became a director of the club in the mid-1960s and remained as a member of the board until the early 1970s.

Dave Woods: Dave grew up watching Wigan and began his career as journalist writing match reports for the *Bolton Evening News* while still at school. After a spell covering the game as a print journalist he has moved on to become one of the game's most popular radio and television broadcasters.

Geoff Wright: A life long Halifax fan, Geoff first visited Thrum Hall while a schoolboy in the 1950s, a decade in which the club enjoyed one of the most successful periods in its history.

Gerry Wright: Gerry grew up watching the great Wakefield Trinity side of the late 1950s and 1960s. He remained a passionate supporter through less successful times in the 1970s and 1980s and when the clubs future was threatened by the proposed mergers which formed part of the initial Super League proposal Gerry became active in the successful campaign to keep Trinity alive. He continues to support the club today.

Appendix 2: 'Ordinary working men... transformed into giants on the rugby field'

(This paper was presented to a postgraduate seminar at De Montfort University in April 2010.)

The 'Up and Under' Rugby League Oral History Project was funded by an internal grant from the University of Huddersfield. The project was run by the University's Centre for Oral History Research and took place over a three year period between 2007 and 2009. Its mission statement was that "By recording and then disseminating the oral reminiscences of the Rugby League community in West Yorkshire – players, officials and spectators – this project will preserve, celebrate and broaden recognition of the sport's rich social and cultural history in the region."

In all the memories of over 100 interviewees were recorded and now form a permanent collection which is held at the University as part of the Rugby Football League Archive. Through the project a website with clips from 26 of the interviews was also created, the inaugural 'Sport and Oral' History Conference was held at the University in April 2009 and a book of extracts from the interviews will be published in autumn 2010.

One of the great strengths of oral history means that the character of this material offers a unique insight into the people, communities and events that have shaped the game. Views have been unearthed which can provide a fresh perspective on major events from those who took part directly or witnessed them as spectators. But perhaps more importantly these oral testimonies also offer an insight into a range of experiences and emotions which would otherwise be left unknown. For as Allessandro Portelli has written "The first thing that makes oral history different... is that it tells us less about events as such than about there meaning. This does not imply that oral history has no factual interest; interviews often reveal unknown events or unknown aspects of known events, and they always cast new light on unexplored sides of the daily life of the non-hegemonic classes."

Due to rugby league's strong association with working class communities, this idea of oral testimony as 'hidden history' is particularly significant. As, amongst others, Richard Hoggart highlighted a lack of literary culture amongst many working class communities has placed great emphasis on oral tradition as a means of preserving and mediating their view of the past. Rugby league's close association with the type of working class communities which Hoggart referred to is reflected in the relative lack of books which have been written about the game in comparison to other sports. Although the situation has improved considerably recently, only a handful of books were written on rugby league in the first 63 years of the sport's existence.

This lack of written history has played a crucial role in the way general perceptions of the game's past have been developed. The type of popular mythology that is often built up around certain events and issues in the history of sport, especially through the informal discourse of supporters, has gained an added significance and led to the construction of a particularly distinctive and powerful self-image.

My aim here is to use extracts from interviews to examine some of the ways in which oral testimony provides an important insight into how popular perceptions of rugby league history have been constructed and can also be used to offer alternative views. To do this, I'm going to focus upon one of many integral facets of rugby league that have been highlighted throughout the project, the fact that, for much of the game's history, professional rugby league players also worked in full-time jobs, often in the communities they represented on the field of play.

For a game that in part owes its very existence to the issue of broken time, the working life of players has clearly had a significant impact upon rugby league. The distinction between open professionalism and broken time payments, in which players were recompensed only for the time they spent away from work through participating in matches, played an integral role in the game's conception.

Clearly, from the outset, it was not intended that rugby league should provide the sole source of income for players. To reinforce this principle a series of 'work clauses' were added to the rules of the game in 1898 which specified that players were required to hold "bona fide employment", which did not include jobs as "billiard makers, waiters in public houses, or any employment in connection with a club." The administrative demands of enforcing the 'work clauses' caused them to be abandoned in 1905. However, the financial realities which faced the game meant that most players had to balance work outside rugby league with the demands of a professional playing career until the 1990s. Indeed, for most professionals who fail to reach the game's highest level, rugby league still offers only a supplementary income to full-time employment outside the game.

But the requirement for players to work in jobs outside rugby league has had an impact which penetrates far beyond the game's economic structure. It helped to create and continually reinforce a strong bond between rugby league players, clubs and the communities they represent which largely remains intact today.

The importance of this relationship to the game's supporters was powerfully reflected in the early memories of Harry Jepson. Harry has given lifelong service to rugby league as an administrator with the Hunslet and Leeds clubs and secretary of Hunslet Schools rugby league, an institution which has produced a wealth of professional players. He grew up in Hunslet in the 1920s and 1930s, and this was the way he explained how his fascination for the game began: "I remember seeing players like, well on this particular occasion it was Jim Bacon who played for Leeds, but there were scores of Hunslet players who worked in the factories. The place was full of factories you see and I thought that's the same chap I saw on Saturday afternoon. I couldn't believe that on Saturday afternoon ordinary working men who wore overalls going down the street were transformed into giants on the rugby field and I was hooked and I don't think I've ever lost that feeling now."

Clearly, this perception of the game and its communal bonds is deeply rooted in the experiences of a man who has had a long and close association with rugby league. Yet, it also reflects how the relationship which was fostered between the player's and supporters of local clubs played a fundamental role in the construction of the game's self-image.

The working life of players outside the game became part the discourse around which a popular conception of rugby league that was based upon an idealised view of traditional northern working class life came to be formed. As Tony Collins has shown, the occupational background of players often mirrored that of predominantly working class communities in which the clubs they represented were based.

So, for example, Stanley Chadwick could write in a 1948 edition of the *Rugby League Review* how, for its supporters, the game "...forms part of their very existence...to them the players are Tom, Bill or Jack; often they work alongside them in workshop or office, and are members of the same club; their wives meet in food queues and at the child welfare centre."

This view was echoed by Geoff Wright who grew up watching Halifax during the 1950s. He recalled how most players "...worked in local jobs, I mean Alvin Ackerley he was a dray man for Whitaker's brewery and when we were going to school Alvin would be there on the dray wagons and we'd see him. You'd see them in the streets. So there was a local affinity because they were working people. Alright they came from Wales, Les Pearce, Ronnie James, Jon Thorley, but they married and made their homes here and they became local people. They were part-time pros but they played in big stadiums, played at Wembley; what a fantastic thing to play at Wembley. Maine Road, Manchester when you could get 50,000 to 60,000 for a Championship final yet they were working alongside you, they worked in engineering shops. I never actually worked with any of the players, but I knew Charlie Renilson very well because he came in the pub. We watched *Match of the Day* on a Saturday night and his wife Thelma and my wife Val they'd be in one corner having a natter and we'd be in the other corner watching ... we were buddies."

Often, the occupations of players reflected the distinctive economic structure of the communities in which the game was played. Perhaps the most famous example of this association between specific industries and rugby league can be found in the coal mining districts of Lancashire and Yorkshire. England international Mick Morgan, who played for Wakefield Trinity, Oldham and Carlisle explained how working in the mines around his home town Featherstone: "At Acton Hall, there was me, Bridgey (Keith Bridges, Featherstone Rovers), Jimmy Thompson (Featherstone Rovers and Bradford Northern), Vince Farrar (Featherstone Rovers and Hull FC), our Arnie (Arnie Morgan, Featherstone Rovers) and lads at Acworth

(Colliery) they had down the pit, there was Dale Fennell (Bradford Northern), Jackie Fennell (Featherstone Rovers), David Hobbs (Featherstone Rovers and Bradford Northern) they all worked at the pit. Everybody worked at the pit, Peter Smith (Featherstone Rovers) worked on the pit top."

The nature of work in which most professional rugby league players found themselves was also important. Most players were employed in manual jobs as skilled, semi-skilled or unskilled labour and this has been equally significant to predominant perceptions of the game.

The cultural world of manual labour was built around a distinctive concept of masculinity that was central to the self-image of working men. It encapsulated notions of strength, endurance, the ability to withstand pain and to triumph over adversity which also came to be seen as fundamental characteristics of rugby league players.

The physical demands of mining have clear similarities with those of playing rugby league. In his autobiography which was published in 2001, some years after the industry had been decimated, former Wakefield player and Castleford coach Dave Sampson explained "Years ago men worked down the pit and came up to play rugby. We don't appreciate this when comparing eras of rugby and making analogies of hard physical labour... the toughness of mind and body was made by repetitive hard work and tough occupations that the people of the past had to endure..."

The career of Frank Wagstaff, which began with Hunslet in the 1930s and ended at Batley in the 1950s, reflected this view. After starting work down the mines at the age of 14, he was employed in the industry throughout his rugby league career and recalled how "during the war I used to work every Saturday morning and play rugby in the afternoon".

But other forms of employment also reinforced the concept of masculinity around which the image of rugby league players has largely been constructed. Lifelong Huddersfield supporter Reg Cannon grew up in the Birkby area of Huddersfield where the great Cumbrian forward Douglas Clarke ran a coal delivery business. Few players had a reputation which conformed more closely to the inherent characteristics of rugby league forwards than Clarke. Also a champion wrestler, he had been a member of Huddersfield's team of all talents, which won all four of games major trophies in the 1913–14 season. But, more importantly, he played in the heroic England team that defeated Australia in the 'Rorke's Drift' test match.

Perhaps more than any other, this event became part of the folklore which is central to the construction of the game's self-image. Despite protests from administrators and players the England side was forced to play its third test match in seven days. Most of the second half was spent without three injured players, one of whom was Clarke who initially played on despite breaking his thumb, but was eventually forced to leave the field after dislocating his shoulder. Yet England held on to win the match 14–6 and regain the Ashes, which they had lost two years earlier.

Now in his 80s, Reg Cannon remembered little about the matches he watched as a boy. But he could vividly recall how, years after his career had finished, Clarke would still regularly lift two full hundredweight bags of coal onto his wagon, one in each hand.

Most players, however, had a very different view of the impact working life outside rugby league had on the game. Rather than focusing on this romanticised view of the bond between players and supporters, their recollections reflect a more diverse range of experiences. Many recalled how balancing full-time employment with a professional career in the game was a considerable challenge. For some, the demands of working life had a detrimental impact upon their playing career. Eddie Illingworth, who played for Batley in the 1950s, for example, worked in a large-scale production industry in which work patterns were structured around shift work. He explained: "I worked nights, 12 hour nights, Humphrey carpets weaving, that was my job and rugby came second... I've come off, Saturday morning six o'clock after starting at six o'clock the night before, five nights a week, come off and go to Hull or Hull Kingston on the bus at 10 o'clock Saturday morning with no sleep when I've done 12 hours on the machines... every week I'd go train, play do me best, 100 percent, you know many times it was how I felt... sometimes you'd feel good if you were on days and training, if I were on nights I didn't feel so good, I just couldn't put that extra in, ... you could look the part but inwardly you're not the same... I think I had the ability, but I just couldn't get that 100 percent fit."

Eddie's career was consequently spent on the fringes of the professional game alternating between the first team and reserves at Batley, one of rugby league's less fashionable clubs.

Those players who enjoyed more successful playing careers, on the other hand, encountered difficulties combining the demands the game placed upon them with regular full- time employment outside rugby league. Trevor Ward explained how the game "took its toll financially" on his father Ernest, who captained Bradford Northern and Great Britain in the 1940s and 50s. He took part in two tours to Australia, and the time spent away from work caused the downfall of his business as a builder. Hunslet international Geoff Gunney encountered similar problems. After serving his time as plumber, he recalled being asked to leave his job "...because I broke too much time to play football. If you got injured, of course, you'd be off work or if you got picked for a trip anywhere you'd say 'I'm having a few days off or I'm having a few weeks off' and I did two tours to Australia when I worked there... they asked me to leave after that."

But there were also clearly advantages to be gained from the status enjoyed by professional players. Only the game's elite were required to take prolonged spells off work to take part in overseas tours and others received a more sympathetic approach from employers. For example, Jackie Blackburn, who played for Featherstone Rovers in the 1950s, worked down a local coal mine. He found getting time off to play "no problem, they were all Featherstone supporters, you see, the manager was a Featherstone supporter."

Nevertheless, the demands of professional rugby league clearly restricted opportunities for players to develop a career outside the world of manual labour and an hourly wage structure. Upon moving to Halifax from his home town Workington, where he started his career, international forward John Henderson explained "I'd to have a job where I could get off to go training. So I worked for Halifax Corporation, labouring, actually, on houses."

But the limitations of the job were not lost on him. He decided to end his career at the relatively early age of 30 and recalled how "The job I had was nothing really with the Corporation so it didn't take anything out of you, you'd no responsibility or anything like that, and the money was accordingly. So I thought I'd better get on with life."

On the other hand Trevor Ward, who himself enjoyed a professional career with Wakefield and Dewsbury, was one of the few players who entered a white collar career. After studying at Art College he became a fine artist, but found his employers were unwilling to allow him time off from work to train and play in matches and he drifted out of the professional game.

The challenges which were presented by combining full-time employment with a career in professional sport clearly meant that players and supporters have viewed the impact this aspect of the game's history has had on rugby league from very different perspectives. Derek Hallas, a centre in the 1950s and 1960s with Leeds, Keighley and Australian club Parramatta, for example, offered an alternative view of the relationship between working life and the concept of masculinity that was inherent in the game. He explained: "The game then, you've got to remember, there were engineers, there were miners, there were dockers, a lot of tough jobs and during the week the foreman told them 'you do this you do that' and a Saturday afternoon, it was their release. You know 'let's go out and hit somebody'. So you stayed out of the way."

Indeed, some of the players who spoke about the relationship they had with supporters in the workplace found that admiration and support were far from unconditional. Ken Senior, who played for Huddersfield and Great Britain in the 1960s and 1970s, explained how the reaction of workmates could provide a strong incentive for players to perform well on the pitch. He recalled: "You didn't like being dropped. Because I used to have to go to work and face them guys working on another machine. I took a lot of stick. A lot of it good banter, like, but you didn't like losing and you didn't like having a bad game."

Similarly, Bak Diabira who grew up in Hull and played for Bradford Northern, Blackpool and Keighley explained how "I worked alongside the supporters and when you had a good game it was nice but when you had a poor game, these guys used to tell you about it. It was good in one way because you were all fighting the same cause, they were supporters and they didn't want you to have bad games ... They'd much prefer to come into work on a Monday morning and pat you on the back rather than kick you up the backside. And you enjoyed it; it made your working week a lot more pleasant when you'd had a good game on the Sunday because for the remainder of the week you were the king in the factory."

Yet although these former players have a much less idealised view of their working lives outside rugby league than that of many supporters, there were also some who recalled events which show how the workplace could provide a context in which strong communal bonds were forged. The harsh environment of the coal mines clearly saw a special relationship develop between professional players and their workmates. Keith Bridges, the Great Britain hooker who began his career with Featherstone explained: "Jimmy Thompson worked with me as well and what we used to do was, if you've ever been to Featherstone, the pit was on one side of the lane and there was a bridge across and Post Office Road was on the other side of the road. When we were on afternoons we used to, in us overalls, nip across the railway line, on to the training pitch... do us training and put us overalls back on and nip back over the railway line and go back to the pit."

When asked if his workmates knew about what they were doing he replied "Oh yeah they knew, yeah. They were all right with it, yeah".

This somewhat understated reply belies the significance of the support their fellow workmates gave these two players. Teamwork was essential on the coal face and very few concessions were given to those who did not fulfil their responsibilities. Yet the preparation these players required in order to perform at their best for the local rugby league club was clearly placed ahead of such concerns. Indeed, according to Mick Morgan similar allowances could be made for players as they recovered from the rigorous physical demands of the game. He recalled how "[The other blokes who worked there] oh they looked after you, yeah. You could always get your head down [and have a sleep] on a Monday if you'd been playing. The speccies [who you worked with] they loved it and that's why they looked after you."

The working life of professional rugby league players outside the game is clearly a complex issue. The memories I have highlighted offer a wide range of perspectives which reflect the diverse experiences and different relationships with the game of those interviewed in a way that serves to underscore the inherent subjectivity of oral testimony as a historical source.

People's perception of the past reflects their own outlook and values which are continually reshaped by the changing circumstances in which they find themselves. But many conventional written historical sources also merely offer an individual's perception of events they have witnessed or experienced. Both need to be examined from a critical perspective if they are to be used to reconstruct and understand the past.

By collecting oral reminiscences, community based projects such as this one bring to light views and experiences which would normally be excluded from the historical process. This material can offer an important insight into the way in which popular perceptions of history are constructed. But perhaps more importantly, the recollections of people with such a wide range of experiences also enable a balanced historical view to be drawn and at times offer new perspectives on sport and its meanings.

Best in the Northern Union

The pioneering 1910 Rugby League Lions tour of Australia and New Zealand

Tom Mather

Tom Mather's fascinating account of the first tour 'down under ' by the British Rugby League Lions, which helped establish the sport in Australia and New Zealand, and gave rugby league an international dimension. Published in 2010 at £12.95. Available direct from London League Publications Ltd for just £12.00 post free. For credit card payments visit www.llpshop.co.uk , cheque payments to PO Box 10441, London E14 8WR, payable to London League publications Ltd. It can also be ordered from any bookshop for £12.95
(ISBN: 9781903659519).

Braver than all the rest
A mother fights for her son

By Philip Howard

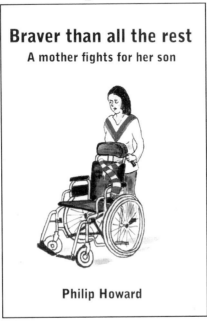

Dave and Sarah Burgess are devastated when their young son Karl is found to have muscular dystrophy. Then another tragedy hits the family hard. But the family are committed to do the best they can for Karl, who has a passion for rugby league. Based in Castleton, a Yorkshire town near the border with Lancashire, Karl's determination to get the most out of life, despite his disability, inspires those around him, in particular Chris Anderton, one of the Castleton Rugby League Club players, who is coming to the end of his career in the game.

Philip Howard is a retired teacher who had responsibility for special needs at a sixth form college. He is a lifelong rugby league fan from St Helens, but now lives near Hull. This is his first novel.

Published in September 2010 at £9.95. Available direct from London League Publications Ltd for just £9.00 post free. For credit card payments visit www.llpshop.co.uk , cheque payments to PO Box 10441, London E14 8WR, payable to London League publications Ltd. It can also be ordered from any bookshop for £9.95 (ISBN: 9781903659526).

Calm in the Cauldron
A rugby league journey
John Dorahy
with Tom Mather

John Dorahy was a great player in
Australia in the 1970s and 1980s. He was
also a successful coach. This
autobiography covers his full career,
including his time in England with Hull KR,
Halifax, Wigan and Warrington.
To be published in November 2010 at £13.95.
Available direct from London League
Publications Ltd for just £13.00. For credit card
payments visit www.llpshop.co.uk , cheque payments to PO Box 10441, London
E14 8WR, cheques payable to London League publications Ltd. It can also be
ordered from any bookshop for £13.95 (ISBN: 9781903659540).

PETER FOX
The Players' Coach

Graham Williams & Peter Lush

Published in 2008, the authorised biography of
one of the game's most successful coaches is
available for just £5.00 direct from London
League Publications Ltd. For credit card payments
visit www.llpshop.co.uk , cheque payments to PO
Box 10441, London E14 8WR, cheques payable to
London League publications Ltd.

Hunslet through and through
Geoff Gunney MBE, rugby league footballer

Maurice Bamford

Geoff Gunney was one of the great players of
post-war rugby league and a stalwart of the
Hunslet club. Former Great Britain coach Maurice
Bamford outlines his career in an authorised
biography published in 2010. Published at
£13.95. Available direct from London League
Publications Ltd for just £13.00. For credit card
payments visit www.llpshop.co.uk , cheque
payments to PO Box 10441, London E14 8WR,
cheques payable to London League publications
Ltd. It can also be ordered from any bookshop
for £13.95 (ISBN: 9781903659465).